D1430869

"If you suspect that you work for a zombie organization, *Building Smarter Organizations* is for you. Crammed full of practical, concrete suggestions from Gordon Vala-Webb's many years of experience, it just might bring your business back to life."

Euan Semple
Author of *Organizations Don't Tweet, People Do*

"Vala-Webb offers new insight behind the forces driving many companies to failure in today's info-accelerated business environment. He has put together a well-structured and cited analysis—the part about email is great. This book is an invaluable resource for savvy organizations determined not to be left behind."

Dan Hauck
CEO, ThreadKM

"Gordon Vala-Webb reminds us that what has worked for organizations in the past can no longer guarantee success in our connected-digital future. In fact, he makes the case that failure to change in our complex, networked, unpredictable global environment will result in significant organizational inefficiencies and detached employees, and in the worst case, the complete failure of the enterprise. *Building Smarter Organizations* offers alternative and pragmatic approaches to delivering the future of the organization."

Dr. Jonathan Reichental
Chief Information Officer, City of Palo Alto, California

"Don't reach for the shotgun just yet—your zombie organization can be saved, and *Building Smarter Organizations* is part of the 'smartened-up' cure."

Ted Graham
Head of Open Innovation, GM

"In this highly engaging book, Vala-Webb packages existing research with novel insights to produce a clear diagnosis of what ails today's 'zombie' organizations. This foundation produces some practical guidance for what leaders can realistically do to awaken their organization's potential for adaptation and survival. Analogies abound and not only entertain, but truly provoke deeper thought (quiz: how is BlackBerry like the person who drove her car into a lake?). But don't be fooled: Amidst the humor and catchy graphics, this book tackles some serious issues such as worker disengagement, unproductive and even dangerous biases, and the misuse of power in organizations. *Building Smarter Organizations* has the potential to unleash some fresh thinking and spark action where it's needed."

Heidi K. Gardner, Ph.D.
Distinguished Scholar, Harvard Law School Center
on the Legal Profession
Author of *Smart Collaboration*

"Gordon Vala-Webb has written an exceptionally well-researched and informative book. It delves to the core of the plight affecting the 21st century economies of the world—zombie organizations. These are organizations poorly adapted to the changes facing the world and which have little chances of survival. In *Building Smarter Organizations,* the reader will learn the path to avoid becoming a stumbling, bloated organization paralyzed by attempts to emulate 20th century best practices, which are of little use for 21st century problems. Through deep and erudite insights, one is able to walk away from this book well-equipped to face the disruptive forces shaking global markets and keep their company alive for the next century—becoming a 'smart' company."

Dr. Evan Shellshear
Bestselling author of *Innovation Tools*

"Gordon Vala-Webb brilliantly draws from the best of management thought to teach us how to awaken our 'zombie organizations' and give them a readiness to sense, reflect, and respond to the technology, competitive, and demographic changes around them."

Katrina Pugh
Academic Director, Columbia University Information and
Knowledge Strategy Program

"*Building Smarter Organizations* offers business leaders a unique insight into how their existing processes and resources limit their ability to rapidly respond to competitive business threats and new market opportunities. Checklists and content in the early chapters help the reader recognize that their organization was designed to compete in a marketplace that no longer exists, and that changing this is tough when current management practices have been developed to ensure efficiency, not innovation. Unfortunately, as the author notes, such practices (around how organizations make decisions, allocate resources, or establish priorities) are of limited value when trying to change the business to address today's challenges. In fact, as Gordon Vala-Webb notes, they can constrain your ability to respond and remain competitive, or even to survive. If you recognize the need to innovate but are struggling to become innovative, I recommend that you read *Building Smarter Organizations*, which offers an innovation road map to help you identify where you are, the challenges you face, and a way forward."

Andrew Maxwell, Ph.D.
Associate Professor, Lassonde School of Engineering, York University
Chief Innovation Officer, Canadian Innovation Centre
Co-founder, Innovation Cartography

"A delightfully cynical takedown of management fads, *Building Smarter Organizations* pulls no punches, takes no prisoners, and tears down the shibboleths of management consultants. It does all of that while being well-researched and easy to read. It offers no magic formula for success, but read it for the good advice it provides on what needs to change, and to learn how to start the change."

Prof. Dave Snowden
Founder, Cognitive Edge
Director, The Cynefin Centre for Applied Complexity,
Bangor University

"Gordon Vala-Webb has written a really fun, imaginative, and informative book in *Building Smarter Organizations: How to Lead Your Zombie Organization Back to Life*. The book has lessons to learn that will help your organization be less like a zombie and more like a living, modern organization. Many, like me, will read the entire book in one sitting because it is easy to read and will make you think of all sorts of ways your organization is rooted in rotting autopilot, devoid of all the processes necessary for a modern, dynamic, information-driven organization."

Brett Trusko
President and CEO,
International Association of Innovation Professionals
Editor, *Global Innovation Science Handbook*

BUILDING SMARTER ORGANIZATIONS

How to Lead Your Zombie
Organization Back to Life

GORDON VALA-WEBB

elevate

Published in Boise, Idaho by Elevate. An imprint of Elevate Publishing.

Print ISBN-13: 9781945449192
eBook ISBN-13: 9781945449260
Library of Congress Control Number: 2016955887

To
Lucia and Kyrie

CONTENTS

PREFACE

Dear reader,

As you read this book, I hope you might laugh out loud and occasionally scribble down a note when you come across a new idea or useful thought. My greatest wish is that, beyond learning and being entertained, you are inspired and enabled to start leading the organizations you are part of (as an employee or leader or volunteer or board member) back to life.

The book will explain why, just when we need smart organizations in our volatile and digitally transforming world, our organizations are like zombies—slow, stumbling, and unpleasant. It will provide you with the three keys to help your organization become smarter, and some practical "how-to" advice on how to start that process of change (it is not as hard as you think it is).

Building Smarter Organizations came about because I have worked in many organizations and had many different roles: as a union staffer, as a leader in an HR-software start-up, as a change maker in large organizations (both public- and private-sector), as a board member and chair in nonprofits, and as a government policy advisor developing new regulatory and legislative requirements for organizations. Throughout these experiences, I was fascinated with how organizations worked. Over and over again I was mystified by how the (mostly) smart people I worked with or for (or faced across the union table) could so frequently make incredibly boneheaded decisions. I was frustrated at the enormous wasted effort (and time and money) that organizations put into meaningless (or, worse, value-destroying) activities or projects. And I was deeply saddened by the unhappiness and frustration I saw in the people working within organizations of any significant size.

It is hard to see what makes a good movie "good": The script, the acting, the direction, the sets, and the special effects all just seem to work together. But it is easy to see where things go wrong for a bad movie (e.g., miscasting Jack Black as a romantic lead[1]— who thought that was a good idea?). It is the same way with organizations—looking at a good (smart) organization, it is difficult to see why it is "good": Somehow the workers and their customers or clients are happy, the company is making money (or, for a nonprofit or government organization, the funding is secure), and there looks to be a long-term future. But, when you look for it, it is easy to see in a bad (zombie) organization how poor leadership, ancient communication technology, and a siloed hierarchy make things go horribly wrong.

I love technology and science. I grew up reading *Popular Mechanics* and so much science fiction that my mother warned me it would "rot my brain." I did nerdy things, like teaching myself BASIC and programing a Univac 1100 to play Mastermind with me back in 1975 (which, in computer terms, is almost like having contributed to some of the first cave paintings). Later in

---

1 *Meyers, Nancy (Director). (2006). The Holiday. Motion Picture. United States: Sony Pictures Entertainment* For more see: http://www.sonypictures.com/movies/theholiday/

life, I went back to school to get a master's degree in the management of technology.[2]

I look around now and see tremendous opportunity—for people and organizations—in the new information and communication technologies that are available to us (or coming soon). I also see huge threats as that same technology inevitably creates new ways of doing things. Author Kevin Kelly—who helped launch and run *Wired* magazine—in his excellent book, *The Inevitable,* says, "We are morphing so fast that our ability to invent new things outpaces the rate we can civilize them."[3]

Finally, in addition to my fascination with organizations and love of technology, I am passionate about making things better; or, to quote from one of my favorite children's books, *Miss Rumphius*, I think it is very important that each of us "must do something to make the world more beautiful."[4] I have no talent for gardening (Miss Rumphius' chosen approach) or visual arts, and very limited musical abilities; so this book is my attempt to contribute by making organizations work better. They underpin virtually everything we do or want to do in this world (including directly making the world more beautiful). If we can make organizations better (smarter), then all of our lives will be better and the world will indeed become "more beautiful."

This book distills what I have learned from a life of work and study as to why so many organizations are slow and stupid (and are unpleasant to work for or interact with); and what we need

---

2   Masters in Management Science (Management of Technology), Faculty of Engineering, University of Waterloo. For more on the program see https://uwaterloo.ca/management-sciences/programs/master-management-science-online

3   Kelly, K.)2016). *The Inevitable.* New York, New York: Viking Press, p. 3.

4   Cooney, B. (1982). *Miss Rumphius.* New York, New York: Viking Press.

to do to make them "smarter." It covers a wide range of topics, including management theory, neuroscience, complex adaptive systems, political theory, enterprise social networking, constructal law, adaptive case management, and "lean" thinking. I have tried to make it both entertaining and useful. Given its breadth, I apologize in advance if you find any particular section superficial—space simply doesn't allow for a deeper examination.

In the first chapter, I lay out the problem—the volatile world we live in where "digital" is changing everything. Chapter Two explains that zombie organizations are fundamentally built from the wrong premise—that the world is largely stable—and why making predictions and bets are so important. Chapter Three looks at the roots of zombie organizations' operating systems (which date back a hundred years). The next chapter provides a diagnostic test that helps identify whether your organization is a zombie already—or in danger of becoming one. Chapters Five, Six, and Seven walk you through the three keys for any organization to become a smart one: mindset, fast-flow communications, and accelerated decision-making. I thought it might be helpful for you to know what the experience of working in a smart organization would be like—this is Chapter Eight (plus some suggestions on how certain key internal functions like HR and IT might change). Chapter Nine offers some practical advice on how you might work to change your organization, with the final chapter focused on you as "leader" and how you might, as an individual, start leading your company back to life.

Now I invite you to begin the dezombification process by turning to the first chapter. And, as in all zombie movies, it is important to stick together; so please click your way over to www.BuildingSmarterOrganizations.com to join our merry band of zombie fighters.

CHAPTER 1
It's a zombie-unfriendly world

We create organizations to serve us, but somehow they also force us to serve them. Sometimes it feels as if our institutions have run out of control, like the machinery of Charlie Chaplin's film Modern Times. *Why we should become slaves to our servants...A society of organizations is one in which organizations enter our lives as influential forces in a great many ways—in how we work, what we eat, how we get educated and cured of our illnesses, how we get entertained, and how our ideas are shaped. The ways in which we try to control our organization and our organization in return tries to control us become major issues in the lives of all of us.*

—Professor Henry Mintzberg[1]

Organizations in postindustrial societies such as ours, particularly big ones, run everything that you depend on. That includes your flight to your next conference or holiday, your neighborhood garbage pickup (don't forget to put it out before you go!), your home protection system, and your "get-me-going" coffee before your flight. Organizations interact with you, with other people, and with each other to deliver the services, the products, the systems, and the infrastructure you need to live your life in relative comfort and ease.

An organizational operating system is the core set of capabilities that underlie all the different functions within an organization: organizational culture (shared set of assumptions held by employees); brand (shared set of assumptions held by those outside the organization); collaborative technologies (for sharing information); organizational structure (for making decisions).

Most of our organizations have an operating system—this core way of thinking and coordinating what they do—which means that they act like zombies:

- Stumbling around and can't run very fast

- Single-mindedly go in the most obvious direction

- Seemingly unable to learn from their mistakes

- Happiest when shambling along in a crowd

- Uncoordinated body movements

- Apparently unhappy

Being a zombie used to be good enough. The world, in fact, used to be zombie-friendly. The ground was relatively flat, there was little competition, and food was plentiful. But now these zombie organizations—and you likely work in one—operate in an increasingly volatile, uncertain, complex, and ambiguous (VUCA) world. You can see this in any news you happen to see in any country—some of the headlines you might have seen recently include: "The Specter of an Accidental China-U.S. War";[2] "Our [Brexit] leap into the unknown threatens both Europe and the world economy";[3] "How America can overcome the challenges of an aging population";[4] "Workers at S. African power utility Eskom strike over pay, supplies stable";[5] and "Sears tanked because the company failed to shift to digital."[6] We are in a period of uncertainty where there is global hyper-competition, new technologies, new consumer and citizen expectations, and new political forces at play at every level—local, national, and global.

At the same time, as the world becomes more VUCA—and as one of the destabilizing forces itself—everything is becoming digitalized and networked. The core of this is an interacting set of new capabilities—mobile devices, cloud storage, "big data" analytics, and social networking technologies. One of the changes that you see is the whole "Internet of things" whereby devices and sensors can talk with each other and with you. One simple example is the sensor in your printer which can "phone home" to talk to its manufacturer, then automatically sends you an email to your mobile phone to ask (while you wait for your flight) if you want to be sent a replacement ink cartridge.

As a result of this digitization and networking, another profound change is occurring in consumer markets in the form of disruption to those who control the distribution of suppliers' goods and services. Ben Thompson has articulated this dynamic in something he calls Aggregation Theory:

> The best way to make outsize profits...is to either gain a horizontal monopoly in one of the three parts [suppliers, distributors, and consumers/users] or to integrate two of the parts such that you have a competitive advantage in delivering a vertical solution. In the pre-Internet era the latter depended on controlling distribution.

For example, printed newspapers were the primary means of delivering content to consumers in a given geographic region, so newspapers integrated backwards into content creation (i.e., supplier) and earned outsized profits through the delivery of advertising. A similar dynamic existed in all kinds of industries, such as book publishers (distribution capabilities integrated with control of authors), video (broadcast availability integrated with purchasing content), taxis (dispatch capabilities integrated with medallions and car ownership), hotels (brand trust integrated with vacant rooms), and more. Note how the distributors in all of these industries integrated backwards into supply: There have always been far more users/consumers than suppliers, which means that in a world where transactions are costly, owning the supplier relationship provides significantly more leverage.

The fundamental disruption of the Internet has been to turn this dynamic on its head. First, the Internet has made distribution (of digital goods) free, neutralizing the advantage that pre-Internet distributors leveraged to integrate with suppliers. Secondly, the Internet has made transaction costs zero, making it viable for a distributor to integrate forward with end users/consumers at scale.[7]

Many kinds of organizations—even public sector ones—are now facing the new threats (or opportunities) that come either directly from such disruption, or indirectly as a result of a shift in customer or client expectations driven by these new digital capabilities and the changes in consumer markets. This need to digitally transform is being driven by an interest in improving customer transactions and relationships, saving costs, driving innovation, and making better decisions.

Another result of the virtually free cost of distributing content, aside from more information being available to us than ever before, is that there is now more knowledge—theories, blog posts, arguments, dissertations—than ever before. And that knowledge is being added at a faster and faster rate as more and more content is made available. For example, back in 1950 medical knowledge used to double every 50 years; it is estimated that, by 2020, medical knowledge will double every 73 days![8]

Now, there are more people to contribute their information or to share their knowledge than ever. As of September 2016, there were 3.675 billion Internet users—or just over half of the

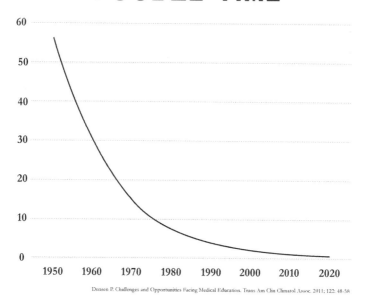

MEDICAL KNOWLEDGE DOUBLE TIME

Densen P. Challenges and Opportunities Facing Medical Education. Trans Am Clin Climatol Assoc. 2011; 122: 48-58

Figure 1: Knowledge being added at faster and faster rate[8]

world's population.[9] And those people can talk with each other (or post a blog or share a video) at ever-faster Internet connection speeds—the global average Internet speed increased by 23 percent in 2015.[10] It is good news that Google has made its mission "to organize the world's information and make it universally accessible and useful,"[11] because we certainly need it.

The third pressure on zombie organizations is that the world economy seems to be entering (or has entered) a period of flat growth. Growth, in an economy, comes from increased productivity; and the United States saw a century of unprecedented improvement between 1870 and 1970 (peaking in the 1950s). Professor Robert J. Gordon argues in his new book, *The Rise and Fall of American Growth: The U.S. Standard of Living Since the Civil War,* that "The economic revolution of 1870 to 1970 was unique in human history, unrepeatable because so many of its achievements could happen only once."[12] There has been a significant reduction in the growth of productivity following this "special century" (at least up until 2014, when the data ends) with a small uptick in the 1990s likely the result of the so-called IT Revolution.

To look ahead, in mid-2016 the former U.S. Federal Reserve Chairman Alan Greenspan pointed to the United States' poor productivity growth and said: "What it's doing is creating a general stagnation in the developed countries which is causing desperation on the part of their electorate" (and gave the U.K. Brexit vote as an example). Greenspan believes that stagflation is heading for the U.S., although the timing of that is unclear.[14] And in a 2016 report, the United Nations Conference on Trade and Development (UNCTAD) warned that, following the previous six years of sluggish growth worldwide, countries could turn more and more to protectionism, triggering "a vicious downward

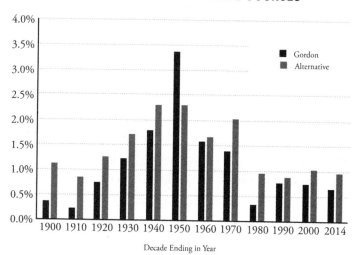

Figure 2: Reduction of U.S. productivity growth[13]

cycle affecting everyone." UNCTAD chief Mukhisa Kituyi said that "Policymakers all around the world face a difficult combination of sluggish investment, productivity slowdowns, stagnant trade, rising inequality, and mounting levels of debt."[15]

So we have a slow-growth, VUCA world increasingly drowning in information and knowledge, with business models that are being disrupted. Most organizations know they need to change. In 2016, by one estimate, 65 percent of large enterprises will have committed to becoming "information-based companies" with an organization focus on "relationships, people, and intangible capital."[16]

The business press is awash with cries for more innovation, articles on how organizations can collaborate more or form partnerships with others, and talk of the latest technology whiz-kid solution.

But the problem is that our existing zombie organizations, which run everything, were built with an organizational "operating system" designed to be effective in a routine, obvious, clear, and simple (ROCS) world; a world where people focused on processes, efficiency, and capital; a world where acquiring and acting on new knowledge and transactions was time-consuming and expensive. In that world—the world of the 50s and 60s—things were rock-solid and resistant to change. What a zombie organization knew yesterday was still going to be (largely) true next year, and the year after that, and likely the year after that as well. As we have seen, a doctor in the 50s could rely on at least half of his or her knowledge being current 25 years after he or she learned it (the trick, of course, was to know which half was still right).

In this ROCS world, new technologies or new competitors did not come along very often—so, for zombie organizations, the focus was on being as efficient as possible. Change was painful, time-consuming, and expensive (zombie organizations hate it); so, without a pressing need for it, organizations focused on doing two things: (1) being really good at repeating the same thing over and over (this was the world of Six Sigma and process re-engineering), and (2) becoming as big as possible so that the organization could achieve economies of scale.

Most people in the ROCS world were doing routine and noncomplex (although perhaps skillful) work. Without digital technology, some of it literally involved pushing paper (at least in carts), and much of it was assembly work in the factory, or routine-based processing of information (or typing or photocopying or assembling it) in the office.

Since the 60s, the world has become increasingly interconnected economically—the results have been a boon to consumers (as prices for many goods have fallen) and increased competition for companies. One sign of the latter—as companies either fold, merge, or are taken over—is the declining average lifespan of a company (listed on the S&P 500), which has dropped from 90 years, in 1935, and is forecast to shrink to 14 years by 2026.[17]

One solution to this increased competition was for zombie organizations to make use of new computer (digital) technologies to either automate the routine work, or to outsource it (or even offshore it). As computers became cheaper, it became more cost-effective to program them to do routine work; even work that required human judgement could be bundled up and sent to a low-cost region. For example, all the Big Four accounting firms routinely have low-level work on audit engagements done in India or another low-wage, English-speaking country.

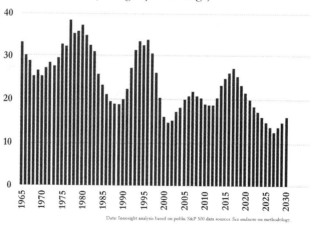

AVERAGE COMPANY LIFESPAN ON S&P 500 INDEX IN YEARS

(rolling 7-year average)

Data: Innosight analysis based on public S&P 500 data sources. See endnote on methodology.

Figure 3: Decline in average lifespan of S&P 500 companies[18]

One major effect of this outsourcing was a shift in the nature of an organization's work. Where previously most of the work in an organization had been routine, now it was complex and required rich interactions with others. A study of the U.S. labor force across all education levels found that the proportion of "nonroutine analytical" and "nonroutine interpersonal" work increased significantly in the U.S. from 1960 to 2009 (as shown in Figure 4), while the proportion of "routine cognitive" has dropped. The turning point occurred around 1970, when the portion of this "nonroutine" work consistently increased while that of "routine" work consistently declined.

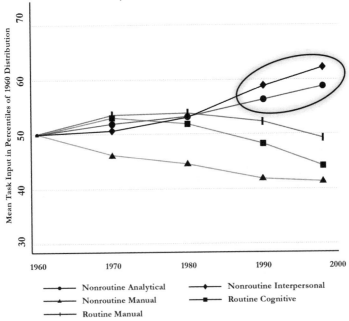

WORKER TASKS IN THE U.S. ECONOMY, 1960-1998:
Autor, Levy, and Murnane (2003) Figure 1

Figure 4: Increase in nonroutine analytical and nonroutine interpersonal work[19]

In another study—which differentiated between "interaction," "transaction," and "production" jobs—we can see that this is a worldwide phenomenon. Interaction jobs make up 41 percent of the U.S. economy and 37 percent in Germany, as one would expect in postindustrial/digital economies; but, even in manufacturing giant China, they make up 25 percent of jobs—and there is such a rapid growth in these kinds of jobs around the world that shortages are expected by 2020.[20] (Although, in a VUCA-digital world, this is difficult to predict.)

So, we have a VUCA world, awash in more and more information and knowledge, with digital disruption occurring almost everywhere. At the same time, since 1970, we have more and more work being automated and/or outsourced, which has steadily increased the portion of the workforce doing nonroutine analytic and nonroutine interpersonal work. And the people doing this work are the kind of people a zombie organization would want to help it figure out what to do next.

In a VUCA-digital world, the agility of an organization is now more important than its size or its ability to repeat what it did yesterday. Jack Welch, CEO of General Electric, once said: "An organization's ability to learn, and translate that learning into action rapidly, is the ultimate competitive advantage."[21] This is true now more than ever—and it poses an existential threat to zombie organizations that are much better at moving in a straight line than dodging the curveballs the world is throwing at them.

"An organization's ability to learn, and translate that learning into action rapidly, is the ultimate competitive advantage."

—Jack Welch

All organizations learn to some extent, and all organizations translate that learning into change; if they were unable to do so, they would have gone under already. But how do organizations "learn" and "translate" their learning into action? And, more importantly, how do they increase the speed at which those two things happen?

The root of both learning and translating learning into action for organizations is the ability to make predictions. Organizations need to improve the quality of the models they use to understand the world today, and become better at predicting what actions they could take to improve their position in the future.

Organizations do this already. Even zombie organizations have a model—often simplistic and unarticulated ("urrgghh")—of how the world today looks to them. They use this to regularly make predictions such as what the sales will be next quarter, what their spending will be by the end of the year, and how many people will be on the payroll next year. Zombie organizations also use this model to make predictions about what courses of actions they should take to improve their future situation. These latter predictions take the form of cost-cutting measures, or new project spending, or efforts to develop new products or services.

But with the world changing so quickly, and knowledge about the world changing so fast, organizations need to have much better models and use them to make much better predictions. And, unfortunately, zombie organizations' operating systems have inherent limits. These limits constrain the ability of people within those organizations to make sense of the world around them, and to make changes that could help the organization, in Spock's words, to live long and prosper.

Sadly, it is not only the organizations that suffer, but also the people working in the organizations. As you can imagine—but as many zombie organizations don't—people doing nonroutine analytical and nonroutine interpersonal/interactive work must be managed differently than those doing routine work. It is difficult to see the work being done and difficult to understand the effort required, not to mention the quality produced. And those doing it expect to use their own judgement, and expect some measure of autonomy.

By continuing to manage them based on a ROCS-world approach, these employees are unhappy and disengaged. According to survey results from Gallup, worldwide, only 13 percent of employees are engaged at work; in North America, 71 percent are "actively disengaged" from their work.[22] How would you know a disengaged worker? They complain, make excuses, lack enthusiasm, don't help others, gossip, lie, are know-it-alls, operate independently, act irresponsibly, don't take initiative, don't ask questions, and are distracted.[23] Does that sound like people you know in your organization? Sadly, it is likely true that, as the comedian George Carlin put it, "Most people work just hard enough not to get fired and get paid just enough money not to quit."[24]

This unhappiness—really, stress—is taking a terrible toll in the workplace. Presenteeism (coming to work, but not really working) alone is costing the U.S. economy a staggering $150 billion (that is billion with a "b") per year;[25] while in the United Kingdom it is estimated that presenteeism is costing the U.K. economy £15.1 billion annually.[26]

One source of unhappiness (stress) for employees, and one source of inefficiency for organizations, is the huge amount of time employees waste on processing email (or being interrupted by it). Highly-skilled knowledge workers—the ones an organization needs to be spending their time understanding and predicting—spend 28 percent of their work week on emails.[27] These emails are part of the continual streams of interruptions that office workers endure. According to one study, office workers are interrupted (or self-interrupted) approximately every three minutes. Bad enough on its own—but terrible when you consider it can take 23 minutes for someone to return to their original task.[28]

So, for leaders of zombie organizations, for those who work in them, and for those who have to interact with them, this book provides answers to these three key questions:

- In a VUCA-digital world, why is the ability to predict the most important ability of an organization?

- What kind of "operating system" does an organization need to be successful?

- How can you do a "hot" reboot of your zombie organization's operating system and give it a new one while it is still running?

If you apply these answers right to your organization, they will give it the ability to sense what is going on around it, decide what to do about it, and change fast enough not just to survive the new world, but to grow and prosper. The people within the organization will align with the purpose of the organization, they'll feel connected with one another, and will engage with their work. Will possess the ability to communicate efficiently across the organization (up, down, sideways) and there are decision-making structures and aids in place to make quick decisions that stick. At that point, your organization is no longer a zombie organization but a smart one.

CHAPTER 2
Zombies can't predict

The paradox of innovation is this: CEO's often complain about lack of innovation, while workers often say leaders are hostile to new ideas.

—Patrick Dixon, Author of *Building a Better Business*[29]

Peter Drucker wrote that the "theory of the business" has three parts:

First, there are assumptions about the environment of the organization: society and its structure, the market, the customer, and technology.

Second, there are assumptions about the specific mission of the organization...

Third, there are assumptions about the core competencies needed to accomplish the organization's mission.[30]

Zombie organizations assume that the environment around the organization is largely stable. As a result, reinforced by years of largely successful experience, zombie orgs make another set of assumptions about the core competencies they need. Basically, they assume that what they need is the ability to repeat—incrementally better—what they did yesterday, based on what they knew yesterday.

This results in an inward focus where organizations are optimized around being consistent and driving lower costs. Where markets are dominated by zombie organizations, the inevitable result is a drift toward commoditization with downward pressure on prices.

In these organizations, the interest is in finding, and applying, so-called best practices:

> Part of the reason for attempting to identify and isolate the single best practice is to eliminate the need to spend time planning what to do. If there is a fully elaborated best practice, then there is no need to waste time planning. Planning is viewed as a waste, and if planning can be eliminated, then workers can spend all the time doing productive work.[31]

In zombie public-sector organizations, or other like organizations that do not face the immediate pressure of a competitive marketplace, best practices are replaced with "most-convenient-for-us" practices (since the elimination of waste is less of a concern than making life easier for those within the organization). In any case, for organizations in the public eye, the fear of media attention drives people to keep doing what they have always done (because it is much easier to defend why you kept doing the same thing, rather than to explain why you changed it to a method that didn't work).

Within those organizations, doing nothing differently—with only incremental improvement—is the best way to be successful. Why? It keeps the organization out of the news and, as a manager, rewards you by maintaining your existing set of positions in your business unit. Making a change might put either of those at risk—which could put your job on the chopping block. In zombie organizations, it is almost as if there is an "innovation killer" org chart that looks like this:

INNOVATION KILLER ORG

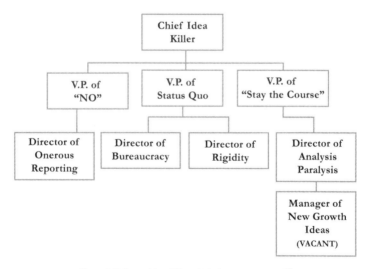

Figure 5: Doing nothing different is the best way to succeed[32]

However, as we have seen, a VUCA-digital world means that, first, there is an enormous amount of information (and misinformation) available about what is going on; and, second, that such

> "A military force has no constant formation, water has no constant shape: the ability to gain victory by changing and adapting according to the opponent is called genius."
>
> —Sun Tzu, *The Art of War* [34]

information will be shifting and changing daily. This new world requires organizations optimized to maneuver with what authors Verjovsky and Phillips define as using "speed, agility, insight, and innovation to win the largest victory at the least possible cost."[33] So, to survive, organizations now need to—in real time—understand what is going on; and to determine whether, and how, to respond to (or take advantage of) this new or emerging environment. In essence, organizations need to be much better at making predictions—and then placing the right bets on those predictions in the form of putting time, attention, and money into making the necessary changes.

These predictions and bets pervade everything an organization does—they are called decisions. It is perhaps obvious that this is the case when an organization decides whether to invest a large sum of money into a game-changing new technology. But hiring someone to fill an existing role is also a set of predictions and a bet. You predict that the role, as currently defined, is required for the foreseeable future; and that the person you hire for the job will be successful in it. And you "bet" time, effort, and—if a recruiter is involved—cash to select, hire, on-board, and train them.

Making accurate predictions is hard. As Yogi Berra famously noted: "It's tough to make predictions, especially about the future." But that is indeed what organizations need to do. Nate Silver, in *The Signal and the Noise,* says this about the problem:

> We have more [information] than we know what to do with. But relatively little of it is useful. We perceive it selectively, subjectively, and without much self-regard for the distortions that this causes. We think we want information when we really want knowledge.
>
> The signal is the truth. The noise is what distracts us from the truth.[35]

To make better decisions (predictions and bets), organizations need to understand, first and foremost, that is what they are doing. Then, organizations need to look for the signal (of what is really going on) amongst all the noise, and to be thoughtful about how they make predictions and bets (i.e., what information is being used, who is involved, which model(s) are being used, how biases are being managed). And then they need to learn from the success (or the failure) of their predictions, and apply that knowledge towards making similar predictions and bets in the future.

As humans, we face a number of challenges in making predictions. First, our brains are optimized to find patterns. That is good and helpful, but it also means that sometimes we find patterns where none exist. There is a reason that the phrase "correlation does not imply causation" is drilled into anyone studying social sciences. For example, the number of people drowning in swimming pools is closely (66 percent) correlated with the number of films that Nicolas Cage appeared in.

Our brain might see that as a pattern—and hope that Nicolas Cage stops making movies.

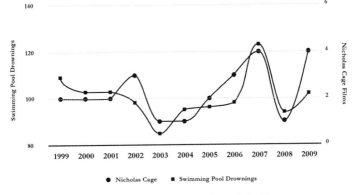

NUMBER OF PEOPLE WHO DROWNED BY FALLING INTO A POOL

(Correlates with films Nicolas Cage appeared in)

Figure 6: Our brains see patterns that aren't there[36]

The other, albeit related, problem, is that when we experience a pattern repeatedly, our brains hard-wire it in (so we can reduce the cognitive load). Professor Coren Apicella explains:

> Whenever you experience something new, your brain responds by firing neurons in specific patterns. If you have the same experience again, the neurons fire in a similar pattern, and if it's repeated enough times, your brain actually creates special, more energy-efficient neural pathways that are like grooves on a well-wrung rug.[37]

Again, a very useful capability to have. We humans use it all the time—when we drive a car along a well-known route, or go to the supermarket to shop (companies work very hard to create these "grooves" in our brain so we buy their products). But this can be a real problem if the original experience you had leads to a false conclusion. "Death by GPS" is a relatively new phenomenon where an experience—that GPS technology works really well—leads people's brains (seemingly) to build pathways such that they overly rely on the device. This results in people using the device ending up in some bizarre, and sometimes dangerous, destinations. Some examples:

- Japanese tourists in Australia drove their car into the ocean while attempting to reach North Stradbroke Island from the mainland

- A woman in Bellevue, Washington, drove her car into a lake that the GPS said was a road

- A Belgium woman tried to go to Brussels, 90 miles from her home, but drove hundreds of miles to Zagreb[38]

Something similar can happen to organizations that over-rely on their internal—but outdated or wrong—GPS, with them ending up dead or in a very uncomfortable location. Some examples:

- Xerox: Invented the personal computer, then fumbled (stock price is now 15 percent of its peak)

- Eastman Kodak: They built one of the first digital cameras—and then did not see the consumer shift from film to digital cameras (bankrupt)

- BlackBerry: Led the way for smart mobile devices—but could not manage to shift fast enough to match consumer tastes (stock price down to 4 percent of its peak)

- Blockbuster: Failed to shift from mail and retail distribution to online (bankrupt)

There is a set of common psychological biases that people bring to decision-making within organizations. These include:

- Confirmation bias: Only looking for, and therefore only seeing, information that reinforces what you already believe (e.g., you believe that alternative technologies are poor substitutes for your excellent product, so you only see information that confirms that)

- Anchoring: Making your prediction based on information you received early on in the process

- Overconfidence: Thinking that you are much better at predicting than you really are

- Sunk-cost fallacy: You have invested so much so far (money, time, effort), that you continue to invest more in order to "save" what you have spent so far

- Gambler's fallacy: You expect that what happened before will influence what happens next (e.g., things have been good for the last 10 years, so you expect things to continue to be good)

"A word of caution: our research shows that CEOs often overestimate their ability to predict and shape their environment, and consequently lead their companies astray."

—Boston Consulting Group

A famous experiment that demonstrates people's propensity to irrationally follow the sunk-cost fallacy is the "dollar auction": As players bid to win a dollar (but where both players have to pay their final bid so the outcome of the auction is framed as a "loss"), players irrationally keep bidding higher and higher (and well past the $1 they are bidding on) to "protect" themselves against losing. During one auction—for $20—in an executive (!) MBA course, the final bids were $2,000 and $1,950![39]

Individuals have these biases, but the culture and structure of a zombie organization can also bake them into organizational decision-making. How many times, for example, have you seen good money chasing after bad (sunk-cost fallacy) even after a project is clearly unsuccessful? A classic example is the Concorde, about which Consultant Peter Saxton, a former RAF pilot and British Airways captain, chief pilot, and senior manager, surmised that the U.K. and French governments kept "throwing more good money after bad" because they "seemed prepared to pay the prestige premium no matter how high it rose."[40] This "escalation of commitment" gives this fallacy its alternate name: The Concorde effect.

The effect is pervasive. A study of non-performing and bad loans at 132 California banks, over a nine-year period, found that where there was turnover in the bank executives, the banks increased their provision for bad loans and wrote more loans off. With the departure of bankers who had originally made the bad loans, the organization was freer to recognize that fact and move on. As the study put it: "People who have reason to defend or justify a course of action would no longer be present to promote such a position."[41]

Overconfidence is another psychological bias you often see played out in zombie organizational decision-making. In a study by the Boston Consulting Group looking at the impact of digital change on companies, the researchers concluded: "The trick is to figure out when you can draw on existing or latent strengths to shape a market and when you need to acquire new capabilities or adapt to ambient forces. *A word of caution: our research shows that CEOs often overestimate their ability to predict and shape their environment, and consequently lead their companies astray.*"[42] [Emphasis added]

So how does a person or an organization make better predictions? You need five things:

- A model—to understand how the world works

- Situational awareness—to see what is happening

- Decision-making (prediction/betting) ability—to decide what to do about what is happening using the model

- Decision-execution ability—to effect the changes that now need to happen

- Feedback loops within, and across, all of these—to learn how to get better

The world is too complicated to understand in its raw form. So, to understand it, you need to build a model of the part of the world that you care about—one that simplifies what is going on enough so that humans can understand it; but that is also "real" enough to be useful in making a prediction. As Professor George E.P. Box once said, "...there is no need to ask the question, 'Is the model true?' If 'truth' is to be the 'whole truth,' the answer must be 'No.' The only question of interest is, 'Is the model illuminating and useful?'"[43] The model has to be a good-enough match to the real world, while simplifying it enough so we humans can understand it to make predictions.

Weather forecasters use rich models combining immense amounts of data to produce their predictions as to whether it will rain tomorrow. Likewise, organizations need "models" to understand how their markets work (or, for public sector organizations, their stakeholders and clients), and how their organizations work.

Often, companies have fairly clear financial models showing where the money is coming in (revenue) and how it gets spent (expenditures). They are used at budget-setting time when organizations look in the rearview mirror to see where the money came from, and was spent, in the last year (or last three or five years). Then they project forward from that, adjusting as necessary to consider anticipated upcoming changes for the year. Each operating unit typically has some sense of "how things work" in their area (whether they can articulate that is another thing altogether); and they try to look ahead to see what might be changing to create a budget for next year.

Unfortunately, in zombie organizations, these different senses of "how things work" across the different business units are rudimentary and not integrated or interconnected in any rigorous way. Even just coordinating next year's work activity and spending is difficult, let alone coming up with a shared understanding of how everything across the firm connects. Leaders and staff of those units spend hours and days in windowless rooms trying to see the connection/collision points, and create Enterprise Project Management Offices to try to find and coordinate the key intersections as much as possible.

And, of course, what the organization does (or doesn't do) has an impact on its customers or clients and competitors and vendors. And vice versa (i.e., what those external actors do has an impact on the organization). So, there is this constant interplay—a complex adaptive system—occurring within the organization, and between the organization and the environment in which it operates. This complex reality is one which financial budgeting and traditional project planning cannot handle.

Of course, after you have a model, you also need to know what is going on—to be aware of the situation you are in. In zombie organizations, staff are typically told to keep their head down and their eyes focused on their work. SMART-goal-based performance management systems—as we shall see later in the book—encourage people to put blinders on and not pay attention to emerging, potentially useful information. In these organizations, scanning the environment is either not done, or is handed to a specialized function (e.g., competitive intelligence), or is limited to only the senior leaders.

In smart organizations, everyone is encouraged to look for emerging information that could be relevant to the organization, and to share it. Furthermore, there are technologies—the replacement of internal email with open-pull social-networking software—and techniques—the visual management through kanban—in place to make the sharing and filtering of information quick and easy. Smart organizations can have much larger numbers contributing to their awareness, because everyone understands the organization's purpose and how their function is aligned to that purpose.

Smart organizations also have decision-making mechanisms to filter and focus attention on the most important new information (e.g., making a prediction as to which competitor is most threatening and should be paid more attention). And they also have the decision-making capability to decide what to do about it. Since there are many more decisions to be made, and made quickly (about where to focus attention and what "bets" to make), smart organizations must have decision-making capabilities that are much faster and more efficient than zombie ones.

Making a prediction (and consequent bet) in a zombie organization is relatively simple. First, you assume that the world tomorrow will be very similar to the world today; and therefore, what worked yesterday will work tomorrow (i.e., the model won't change). Standardized processes are preferred to open and "messy" ones. For example, if someone leaves a zombie organization, the standard process would be to recruit as quickly as possible so that there are no empty positions on your org chart (with the fear that, if the position is not filled quickly, someone else might arbitrarily eliminate it as a "cost savings").

Alternatively, someone like the CEO or another senior leader reads a magazine article about something, and decides "that is what we need to do." And then the organization works to "make it so" as per *Star Trek: The Next Generation*'s Captain Picard. So, we have two models of decision-making in zombie organizations: Either repeat old decisions, or execute on the idea of a powerful single leader (both with little regard to what is happening more broadly). To get a decision made outside of those two models is difficult, time consuming, and frustrating.

In contrast, smart organizations make the assumption that tomorrow could be quite different from today; and that what worked yesterday may not work tomorrow (or that a better way has been developed). The assumption in smart organizations is that the model—for the organization and the environment—is constantly changing. So, if someone leaves a role, the manager of the unit would consider whether that role is still required going forward; perhaps the needs in that area are increasing and the organization should hire two people. Or the work has become more complex, and a more senior person is required. Or automation is available so no one is needed.

But trying to be aware of everything that could possibly have an impact on the organization (situational awareness), and constantly rethinking every scenario (dynamic adaptation)—rather than assuming things haven't changed that much and that the answer is the "tried-and-true"—is exhausting for zombie organizations. This is because zombie organizations have operating systems with a number of key flaws.

First, looking outside the organization to build situational awareness tends to be concentrated higher up the hierarchy, so there are fewer people to do an ever-increasing amount of work. Second, sharing information—particularly across silos—is typically fraught with barriers:

- People don't know who to send the information to

- It takes time/effort that has a high likelihood of being unrewarded

- There is a real (or perceived) risk that the act of sharing might be seen negatively:

  o At the very least, as unnecessary and contributing to information overload; or

  o At the worst, as being "wrong," which calls into question the judgement of the sender

"No one really wants to rethink the basic strategy, which is usually some version of 'do what we did yesterday, but +/- 10 percent here or there.'"

Typically, such cross-silo information-sharing about emerging issues or opportunities happens in a zombie organization briefly as part of some sort of annual (if the organization is lucky) strategic-thinking, planning, or review process. These processes tend to be more form than substance, especially since no one really wants to rethink the basic strategy, which is usually some version of "do what we did yesterday, but +/- 10 percent here or there." Of course, some cross-silo information-sharing about external realities does happen through peer-to-peer connections as part of people's personal networks. But the volume of information is low, there is no way to collect and cross-connect it, and the whole thing is unfocused, ad hoc, and episodic.

Better exchange of information across silos is clearly part of making better organizational predictions and bets, as is accelerating the pace of decision-making and decision-executing. Perhaps more important than either information flow or decision-making is that smart organizations are constantly seeking feedback on how well their bets are paying off, and trying to get better at making them. The era of "big data" is upon us, and will help. What is most important, however, is an organizational culture that focuses on the importance of getting better at finding that signal (about the truth of what is going on and what works) from all the noise that is out there.

Zombie organizations have a "little boxes" mindset, where everyone is supposed to stay within their part of the org structure, not exceeding their level of authority, and within the established best practices. Furthermore, in these organizations, trying something that doesn't work is the surest way of getting sidelined in your career (or fired). In smart organizations, trying something new (within appropriate parameters) is valued—even if the thing didn't work—because it is the only way to find out new stuff. Smart organizations have a mindset of intersecting circles where everything is connected to everything else.

We will see in upcoming chapters how these three components of a smart organization's operating system—fast-flowing communications, accelerated decision-making, and an open mindset—work, and how an existing organization can be rebooted to put them into place. The challenge for zombie organizations is immense. Their world is no longer stable and slow-moving, where success came from focusing on efficiency and scale, and where processes and projects could follow a step-by-step linear sequence. Now, the VUCA-digital world requires a business transformation. Dan McClure, Innovation Design Lead at the consulting firm ThoughtWorks, describes the problem this way:

> Their challenge is discovering and building new ideas while the market rushes forward around them...Traditional plans and control structures are inappropriate for this environment. Pretending that opportunities can be defined up front, clearly evaluated, and remain stable, all while a step-by-step business process runs its course, ignores the reality of changing markets. There are too many unanswered questions, complex interactions, and shifting needs. Instead, the enterprise must become radically more responsive.[44]

Start-ups simply begin with the new operating system already in place; it is quite a different thing for zombie organizations, who must keep running under the old operating system while, at the same time, reinventing themselves with a new one.

This trick—of being both stable and agile at the same time—is entirely possible. A study by Professor Rita Gunther McGrath found that high-performing companies (i.e., those that had increased their net income by at least 5 percent annually for 10 years) were able to keep certain organizational features stable while also having the ability to adjust, and readjust, their resources quickly. This ability to be both stable and flexible, to fully exploit current ways of operating while innovating to create new ones—at the same time—is key to being a smart organization.[45] It requires being able to accept that there is no "right" answer, but two "rightish" answers interdependent of one another (e.g., structure and flexibility, stability and change, control and freedom). This requires organizations and their leaders to manage these polarities.[46]

CHAPTER 3
The roots of the zombie organization

...for the past 50 years, we've run most organizations and some societies along the superchicken model. We've thought that success is achieved by picking the superstars, the brightest men, or occasionally women, in the room, and giving them all the resources and all the power. And the result has been just the same as in William Muir's experiment [with chickens]: aggression, dysfunction, and waste. If the only way the most productive can be successful is by suppressing the productivity of the rest, then we badly need to find a better way to work and a richer way to live.

—Author and Entrepreneur Margaret Heffernan[47]

The zombie operating system has its roots in a mash-up between what Weber called "monocratic bureaucracy" and Frederick Taylor's "scientific management" approach to organizing work. The combination—with the "bam, kick-it-up-a-notch" addition of patriarchal society—was very successful in its day. But, as we have covered in previous chapters, this approach has outlived its usefulness in our VUCA-digital world.

Monocratic (the word sounds so close to "monarchy") bureaucracy has some key features that we largely take for granted in many of our organizations today:

- Fixed division of labor

- Hierarchy of offices

- Set of rules governing performance[48]

Scientific management—or Taylorism—took Weber's idea of a "set of rules governing performance," and, in the industrial age, applied it to organizational work to the ultimate degree. The approach can perhaps pithily be described as "best practices on steroids." Taylorism assumes that the work is repeatable, that there is a best way to do it, that workers are not highly educated (and therefore can only do simple tasks), and basically can't be trusted to do anything without close supervision. The main elements of the approach include:

- Time studies (literally using a stopwatch to time workers as they perform a task to find the fastest way to do something)

- Functional or specialized supervision

- Standardization of tools and implements

- Standardization of work methods

- Separate planning function

- Management by exception principle

- The use of "slide rules and similar time-saving devices"

- Instruction cards for workmen

- Task allocation and large bonus for successful performance[49]

If you replaced "slide rule" with "laptop," "instruction cards" with "corporate portal," "workmen" with "staff," and made it "successful performance *achieving SMART goals*," you likely will recognize your own organization in the elements above. Yes, it is true: The roots of the zombie organizational operating system—and therefore the operating system for most modern organizations—are from the dawn of the industrial era over 100 years ago.

And, to make it worse, these organizations—as all of us do—operate in a society stewed in patriarchy. As Professor Philip Cohen put in his *The Atlantic* article, "America is still a patriarchy":

> In fact—my interpretation of the facts—the United States, like every society in the world, remains a patriarchy: They are ruled by men. That is not just because every country (except Rwanda) has a majority-male national parliament, and it is despite the handful of countries with women heads of state. It is a systemic characteristic that combines dynamics at the level of the family, the economy, the culture, and the political arena.
>
> Top political and economic leaders are the low-hanging fruit of patriarchy statistics. But they probably are in the end the most important—the telling pattern is that the higher you look, the maler it gets.[50]

Philip Slater, in his book *The Chrysalis Effect*, describes modern societies as having a "controller culture," where "controllers" don't "see misfortune simply as a problem to be solved. His first

"Short-term thinking, blame-laying, silos, controllers, bureau-cracy, best-practicism, SMART goals used to identify 'high performers,' and planning-separated-from-doing—these are the hallmarks of a zombie organization."

thought is to find out who to blame." Note the deliberate use of the male pronoun. Does that sound like any of the CEOs, or other C-suite leaders, you have had to work for or with? As a kicker, later in the book, he says: "Decaying institutions are characterized by short-term thinking."

Short-term thinking, blame-laying, silos, controllers, bureaucracy, best-practicism, SMART goals used to identify "high performers," and planning-separated-from-doing—these are the hallmarks of a zombie organization. We will see, in the next chapter, how to calculate your organization's "Z" score (i.e., the degree to which the operating system has been taken over by the zombie virus).

Granted, in the conditions organizations faced in the early industrial era, this was an effective operating system. And what were those conditions? There was a poorly-educated workforce, doing repetitive work, making products that changed relatively slowly from year to year, which were being sold into markets with similar competitors using similar technologies. This was an age of standardization—including, even, the standardization of time. Until time zones were invented and agreed upon, railways had trouble operating because each town (east or west) basically had its own time zone (based on a different "noon" when the sun was directly overhead). Standardization accelerated greatly during World War II, and peaked in North America during the 50s and

60s with the automobile age and the big three auto manufacturers (Volkswagen? Honda? Hah! Never!). Unprecedented productivity growth was the order of the day—and people's standards of living (at least in the Western industrialized world) grew with it. During this period, organizations strove to build economies of scale and to reduce waste. Remember, according to Taylor, planning is wasteful, which is why he believed a company should find a "best practice" and stick to it. Starting in the 70s and 80s, as more competitors entered different markets and globalization began, organizations began to feel increasing pressure to do more with less (without ever considering rethinking their operating system).

A form of ultra-Taylorism developed—aided and abetted by consulting firms both big and small—with their constellation of approaches and acronyms. My nominees[51] for the Hall of Fame for Management Fads Gone Wrong[52]—Ultra-Taylorism category—would include:

- Business process reengineering (BPR): Focus on improving workflows and business processes to cut costs and improve customer service

- Six Sigma (6σ): This is ultra-business-process reengineering whereby you find and eliminate all deviations from the norm. Six Sigma refers to a process "in which 99.99966 percent of all opportunities to produce some feature of a part are statistically expected to be free of defects"[53]

- Balanced Scorecard (BSC—but should be BS): semi-structured measurement and reporting, so that managers can track execution of activity and the outputs

Then, as it became obvious these weren't working very well, there were attempts to mitigate the worst effects by yet more management fads. One that I thought was blindingly obvious (and which I can't believe anyone actually paid for) was Management By Walking Around (MBWA)—which is exactly what it sounds like. A very strong contender for the Hall—in the Mitigating the Worst of Taylor category—would be Matrix Management. This fad, adopted by many organizations, directed an organization to change its structure so that workers reported up the chain of command (again, notice the language we use: "chains" and "commands") to not *one* but *two* "controllers" (a.k.a., managers). The thinking was that, if the stacked one-head model (i.e., hierarchical organization design) wasn't working, then the stacked two-head design must be better. Here is the rationale for the fad as described in the *Harvard Business Review* article "Matrix Management: Not a Structure, a Frame of Mind" from 1990:

> The obvious organizational solution to strategies that required multiple simultaneous management capabilities was the matrix structure...Its parallel reporting relationships acknowledged the diverse, conflicting needs of functional, product, and geographic management groups and provided a formal mechanism for resolving them. Its multiple information channels allowed the organization to capture and analyze external complexity. And its overlapping responsibilities were designed to combat parochialism and build flexibility into the company's response to change.[54]

The same article goes on to describe why the approach was a colossal failure:

> In practice, however, the matrix proved all but unmanageable—especially in an international context. Dual reporting led to conflict and confusion; the proliferation of channels created informational logjams as a proliferation of committees and reports bogged down the organization; and overlapping responsibilities produced turf battles and a loss of accountability. Separated by barriers of distance, language, time, and culture, managers found it virtually impossible to clarify the confusion and resolve the conflicts.[55]

A slow retreat from matrix management ensued. But the increasing pressure from competitors was relentless. New management approaches emerged in the 90s like knowledge management (KM)—a softer, kinder Taylorism that centered on codifying knowledge and standards and making those easier for people to browse (and later search), so they could become more efficient. The classic encapsulation of this approach is found in what became a KM aphorism: "If HP only knew what HP knows,"[56] which was popularized by Leo Platt, the CEO of Hewlett-Packard at the time. In the ideal world of the Orwellian-named "Knowledge Manager" during that era (the 90s and 00s), everyone would write down everything they knew in case someone else, later, needed to learn it. This "codification of knowledge" approach—with knowledge portals and intranets for distribution of same—were the order of the day for many organizations; the essential purpose was to improve operational efficiency through the reuse of existing knowledge.

Meanwhile, another very strong contender for the Management Fads Gone Wrong Hall of Fame must be the old canard "performance by objectives." If there was a "confession of faith" for anyone working in an organization, if there were a business leaders' version of a creed or shahada, surely it would include SMART goal setting. It would go like this: "I believe in the power of Specific, Measureable, Achievable, Realistic, Time-based (SMART) goals to drive behavior and boost performance." The problem is that it isn't true. Or rather, it is true about trivial, well-understood things, but not true for anything where you are required to collaborate, be creative, or connect with other human beings in a world that is uncertain and unpredictable, in order to do complex and/or novel things.

In a woeful illustration of the negative effects of SMART goals, you can look at the Ford Pinto. Specific goals for the design of this new car resulted in a car that would easily catch fire in a rear-end collision. Even after the design flaw was found, Ford executives remained committed to their goal. They calculated that fixing the car would cost more than simply paying the costs of the resulting lawsuits (the cost of the car being one of their SMART goals).

In a wonderfully-named Harvard Business School working paper, "Goals Gone Wild," Professor Lisa D. Ordóñez and her colleague authors suggest that the SMART goal systems should really come with this warning label:

⚠ WARNING

Goals may cause systematic problems in organizations due to narrowed focus, unethical behavior, increased risk taking, decreased cooperation, and decreased intrinsic motiviation.

Use care when applying goals in your organization.

Figure 7: Warning - Goals gone wild[57]

Unfortunately, in the Taylor-inspired zombie organizations, this warning is largely unknown, let alone heeded.

The "corporate kabuki"[58] of the performance review process—a highly-ritualized performance whereby everyone is rated from high-performer to non-performing based on their achievement of their SMART goals—is hated by everyone who participates in this sham. Judging employees with ratings and write-ups—like restaurant reviews[59]—destroys value in many ways: It deters people within zombie organizations from collaborating (if it is not on my list of SMART goals, why would I work to help you?); it inhibits learning (since being judged triggers a fear-fight response); it limits innovation (since SMART goals focus on performing quantifiable things that can be identified one year or more ahead); and it lures people into unethical behavior (e.g., the Ford Pinto, the Enron/Anderson scandal,[60] and the Veterans Affairs Hospitals fiasco[61]). Finally, a few firms—Accenture and Deloitte being the latest and biggest[62]—are dropping these systems, but these are very much exceptions to the zombie organization rule.

Another part of the Zombie Organization Manager's creed includes managing around the average: "Everyone can be understood by using a bell curve; you can define Average Workers—and thus find High Performers; and a one-size approach to people *does* fit all." The purpose of doing so is to drive efficiency:

> Performance appraisals that follow a normal distribution and that compel employees to be force fitted in a bell-shaped curve are efficiency-focused. Such human capital management tools are utilised to contain cost, boost efficiency, and increase the bottom line of the firm.[63]

But people's performance within an organization does not map to a bell curve (also known as a "normal," or Gaussian, distribution) where you have a few good performers, a few bad ones, and most others in the middle.

GAUSSIAN DISTRIBUTION

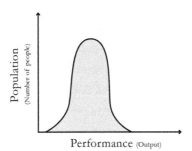

Figure 8: Performance curve - Normal distribution[64]

Instead, there is much evidence to suggest that the distribution of performance within an organization more closely fits a "Paretian" (or power law) distribution (from whence comes the Pareto principle's 80/20 rule). The main study, conducted in 2012 by O'Boyle Jr. and Aguinis, found this Paretian distribution of performers repeated over and over again in 198 samples, over more than 633,000 people, and across many different settings including academia, politics, and sports. Here's what that distribution looks like:

PARETIAN DISTRIBUTION

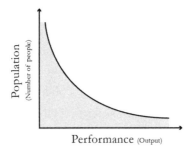

Figure 9: Performance curve - Power law distribution[64]

MISSED SUPERSTARS

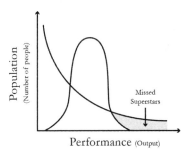

Figure 10: Misunderstanding the distribution of performance[64]

Thinking the distribution is around the average, when the distribution is actually Paretian, leads zombie organization managers and HR people to make a couple of mistakes. First they miss a large number of "superstars" (see the figure above). How much does this matter? The O'Boyle Jr. and Aguinis study found that the very top 5 percent of staff outperformed the average ones by 400 percent in most companies![65]

The other mistake that zombie organizations make, by following the nonexistent bell-curve distribution of performance, is to assume there is a big lump of people in the middle who are more or less close to the average. As you can see on the charts above, there is no bulge in the middle where most people—rated "Meets Expectations"—are located. Instead, the difference between a high-middle performer and a low-middle performer is significant. In zombie organizations, these people are largely treated the same, with similar bonuses and with little extra attention or development opportunities.

Dr. Rose, in his book *The End of Average*, points out that no one is average:

> Human beings don't line up perfectly. There is no average learner. They have strengths and weaknesses. They all do. Even geniuses do.[66]

Zombie organizations strongly believe in the myth of an "average" person when, instead, we vary considerably along any set of attributes we might have. We are, in fact, all "jagged" with low, average, or high abilities in memory, language, curiosity, and cognition.

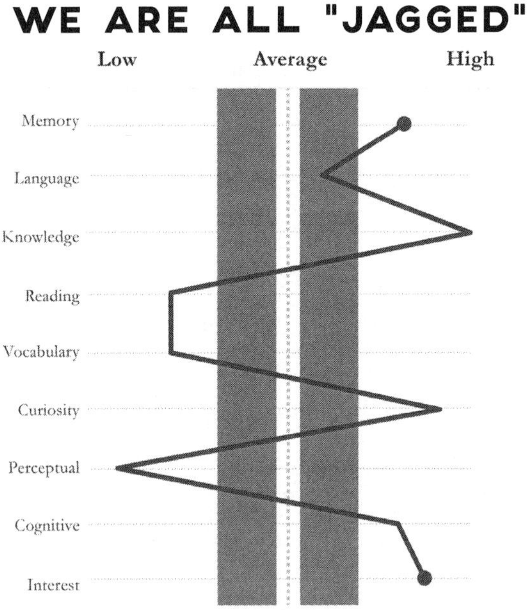

WE ARE ALL "JAGGED"

Low	Average	High

Memory
Language
Knowledge
Reading
Vocabulary
Curiosity
Perceptual
Cognitive
Interest

Figure 11: Myth of the average person[67]

The combination of annual SMART goals with "restaurant rating" of staff, erroneously using a bell-curve distribution of talent, means that zombie organizations destroy value through their performance management systems. Is it little wonder then, that the Corporate Executive Board (CEB) says they are "a burdensome process that encourages fear and uncertainty...[with] no correlation between business unit success in hitting profit goals and performance management scores—if anything, the data show a tiny negative correlation"?[68] CEB says that two-thirds of actual high performers are not rated as such by their organizations.[69] So you will not be surprised to learn that CEB surveys have shown that 95 percent of managers are dissatisfied with their systems, and 90 percent of HR leaders do not believe they provide accurate information.[70] The real wonder is why organizations continue to use them. Some companies—such as GE, the Gap, and Adobe Systems—have now dropped their annual reviews and ranking systems for just these reasons.[71]

The work of predicting, in a VUCA-digital world, is most definitely nonroutine and many times complex. It requires you to be creative, to be aware of other people and the impact you have on them, and to be collaborative. In zombie organizations, it is assumed that everyone is fundamentally rational in how they operate, and that we are individuals first (and social beings second). The zombie organization management creed would contain this doctrine: "Humans are thinking, rational, and individual animals, who sometimes feel, and sometimes bond together, as well."

The latest evidence from neuroscience strongly suggests otherwise. Jill Bolte Taylor, a Harvard neuroanatomist who suffered a stroke and wrote about her brain's recovery, says:

> Although many of us may think of ourselves as thinking creatures that feel, biologically we are feeling creatures that think.[72]

And, as Director of the NeuroLeadership Institute Dr. David Rock put it:

> The human brain is a social organ. Its physiological and neurological reactions are directly and profoundly shaped by social interaction.[73]

As "feeling creatures" with brains that are a "social organ," when we are judged as part of a performance review, or when we are blamed by a "controller" for something that went wrong, or when we fear we could lose our job (and be forced out of our work community), we perceive a threat. Our body's fear-flight response kicks in as our bodies react automatically by releasing adrenaline. Blood flow to our limbs is increased, while we lose access to our social engagement system (in our limbic brain) and our brain's executive functions (in our prefrontal cortex). Basically, what happens is that "the higher the level of stress hormones, the more primitive the brain becomes in its thinking, moving from thinker toward snake."

Of course, we are attracted to things as well (like eating fat and sugar or connecting with others). However, we humans tend to pay more attention to things that frighten us compared to things that we like. From an evolutionary perspective, this overweighting of threatening things was obviously a useful kind of hedge: Really bad things might happen to you if you get it wrong (e.g., getting eaten by the tiger in the bushes), and that the best thing you could hope for would be to get something to eat yourself (e.g., the fruit on those bushes). The reactions we humans now have, based as they are in fear or attraction, are no longer triggered by tigers or fruit. They come, instead, as a result of the social dynamics that surround us.

David Rock has developed the SCARF mnemonic device to help us remember the key ones:

SCARF MODEL OF SOCIAL THREATS AND REWARDS

Figure 12: SCARF model of social threats and rewards[74]

In Rock's model, the social Away-Toward elements are rank-ordered so that, for example, Status is the most important trigger; while Fairness is the least important one. When you apply the SCARF model, you can easily see how a SMART-goal performance ranking system would drive people to have threat responses:

- Status threat: "I don't want to be given a low rating."

- Certainty threat: "This process doesn't make sense."

- Autonomy threat: "I don't want to fill out these forms and go through this process."

- Relatedness threat: "I like my boss and co-workers; but now it feels like I have to be game-playing in a win-lose situation."

- Fairness threat: "Why is he a '1' and I'm not?"

If people don't feel safe, their ability to interact socially and their ability to make judgements become impaired. People, under threat, literally become zombie-like: unable to relate to others and unable to think rationally. In the worst of zombie organizations, people working within them are constantly in a state of worry (i.e., they perceive a constant, low-level threat to themselves). Even if nothing else in the zombie organization's operating system reduced the organization's ability to function, this would.

One final irony for a zombie organization's operating system is that the high-performing staff need the others around them to be successful. Superstars, or superchickens, need others. William Muir, an evolutionary biologist, looked at the productivity of six generations of average chickens when they were just left alone. He compared that flock's productivity to a flock of superchickens that he had created by choosing only the most productive chickens over six generations. By the end, the flock of average chickens was healthy and their egg production was up dramatically; the superchickens, however, were in a sorry state with only three of them left (they had pecked the others to death).[75]

If you think this concept only applies to chickens, you may be a bird brain. In a study of over 1,000 "star" stock analysts working for 78 investment banks, the researchers found: "When a company hires a star, the star's performance plunges, there is a sharp decline in the functioning of the group or team the person works with, and the company's market value falls." The study concluded: "An executive's performance depends on both her personal competencies and the capabilities of the organization."[76]

Does your organization have the right capabilities to help your superchickens soar? Remember—there are considerably more of them than you thought. Or do you work in—or lead—a zombie organization? And, how would you even know? In the next chapter, we will give you an easy-to-apply test that you can use to calculate your organization's "Z"—or Zombie—score. Then, you will get some practical advice for how to reboot your organization with a new operating system that does help chickens to fly. The bottom line? "When a firm operates in a dynamic environment, a solitary focus on bottom line leads to dysfunctional consequences for the long-term sustenance of firms."[77]

CHAPTER 4

Zombies eat brains: How to know if your organization is a zombie

Does anybody drive staring at their rearview mirror? You know that if you did that over a period of time, you would eventually crash. The tough stuff is in front of you—the shift to mobile, for example. It's like ice forming on the road, and you don't want to miss it. You may be in the wrong car. Maybe you need to pull over and put on some snow tires.

—Caryn Marooney, VP of Tech Communications, Facebook[78]

Zombie organizations that continue to use their operating system from 100 years ago are all around us. They are so numerous, and their operating systems so common, that we think of them as "normal." In their dysfunction, it is shocking there still are so many!

I think the reason for their current dominance is that the infection is so widespread that the competitive pressure on any individual zombie organization is reduced. The old adage applies here: You don't have to be the fastest runner when a bear is chasing a group of you, merely faster than the slowest member. So, if all the organizations are zombies, you can still remain a zombie and be relatively successful in your chosen niche as long as you are not the slowest zombie being chased by the VUCA-digital bear.

Another reason for zombie dominance is that, while there has been global competitive pressure for decades, the impact of the world becoming digital is relatively new. That combination—of globalization and digitization—is only now putting massive pressure on organizations. The degree of pressure varies tremendously from industry to industry; for example, the media industries have seen, and continue to see, enormous changes that started over 10 years ago (YouTube was only founded in 2005, and Netflix only started streaming movies in 2007). Other industries, like professional services, for example, have seen much less change—although new technologies, including AI, promise to bring disruption to lawyers and accountants.

Organizations come in all shapes and sizes, but, generally, they are more likely to have zombie operating systems if they are:

- Larger (as rules are used to replace aligned judgement)

- Older (as the internal systems were created in a time where standardization and hierarchy worked)

- More protected in their market (e.g., monopolies and oligopolies) or sphere of operation (like many governmental bodies).

Of course, almost no modern zombie organization could survive if the full company had gone completely zombie; if so, it would have been taken over by some less zombie-ish organization. So, every zombie organization has within it (perhaps buried deeply) non-zombie elements that offer some flexibility to the organization. And, as we have seen in the previous chapter, there have been some efforts to mitigate the worst tendencies of the Taylorist-Monocratic bureaucracy operating system. We see this in things like slogans (e.g., "There is no 'I' in Team") and posters on the wall (usually, at least in North America, of eagles soaring), or actual programs (e.g., "team building" exercises where teams face some challenge together such as ironically being locked in a box—a current popular choice) so they supposedly learn collaboration-enhancing behaviors.

It may be hard to see directly to the zombie organization's heart through this fog of leadership messaging, program acronyms, and genuinely nice people (at least some of them) in leadership roles. The question you must ask yourself is this: Are you working in, or leading, a zombie organization? How far gone is it?

To help you answer this question I have developed a zombie-organization litmus test that will give you some idea of the degree to which your organization has turned zombie. Think of this test—the "Z" score—as a frontline screening tool to help you identify if your organization is infected, and how far gone it is.

To calculate your organization's "Z" score, answer the questions on the next page. I will explain each one of the sections and elements.

"Z" SCORE

Place "True" or "False" in the column with your answer

Category	Thinking of the behavior you see most frequently within your organization, is this statement true or false?	True/ False
Mindset/ Engagement	Leadership prefers spouting slogans to dealing with reality	
	Most people here are hoping to work somewhere else	
	We infrequently learn from our mistakes	
	People do not trust each other much here	
Communica- tion	There are too many emails and other internal communications	
	People do not know what is going on across our organization	
	It's hard for someone to get useful feedback on their ideas	
Collaboration/ Decision- making	Coordinating work with people in other parts of the organization is hard	
	It is easy to get to a "No" decision, and hard to get a "Yes"	
	Meetings here are useless and unproductive	
Total	*(Count the number of "True")*	/10

Calculating your "Z" score

Your "Z" score is the number of "True" answers. Here is what your score means:

0:     ALL CLEAR: Your organization is not a zombie, and has a "smart" organizational operating system.

1-3:   CONGRATULATIONS: Your organization is not a zombie—beware, though; there is a bit of zombie virus loose in your operating system.

4-6:   DANGER: Your organization is on the cusp of becoming a zombie; you must reboot your organization's operating system as soon as possible to survive in our VUCA-digital world.

7+:   EMERGENCY! Your organization is in full-fledged zombie mode, and drastic action is required immediately (it may be too late, but getting your leadership to read this book will start you on your recovery).

The test is divided into three sections: Mindset/Engagement, Communication, and Collaboration/Decision-making. These sections make up the key components of any organization's operating system. When they are compromised, as in zombie organizations, we see the classic signs of a zombie: the shambling and uncoordinated movements, the fixed stare, very short-term thinking, and the mindless pursuit of one goal (operational efficiency) without being mindful of other opportunities or costs or consequences, and generally the inability to recognize what is going on in the environment and make any significant changes in the organization.

Mindset/Engagement
Leadership prefers spouting slogans to dealing with reality

There is an ancient Greek proverb that says: "The fish rots from the head down." As social animals, we take our cues for how to behave and what to do from our leaders. Their way of thinking will permeate an organization, even if their way is "rotten." Leaders, by their words—and especially by their actions—create and shape the environment that, in turn, creates and shapes all the predictions and bets made by all the people in the organization.

When leaders—as we see in zombie organizations—focus on criticism, fault-finding, and doublespeak, the result is an organization where innovation, exploration, and creativity are limited. This shows, as Carol Dweck has framed it in her book *Mindset*, an organizational mindset that is "fixed." In such organizations, employees believe only a handful of "star" employees are valued highly.[79] Of course, the leaders of these organizations, and the other leaders they chose, consider themselves to be among that handful. These elites are self-replicating—they only promote and reward others like themselves (or those who are good at masking themselves to look like the elites); and are self-referential, looking only to each other for confirmation that they are doing the right thing.

Consequently, these elites lack diversity both in their make-up (i.e., gender, race, background) and in the repertoire of perspectives to which they have access. Is it no wonder that the rate of psychopathy amongst senior business leaders is three to four times that of the general population?[80] As Paul Babiak and Robert Hare put it in their marvelously titled book, *Snakes in Suits*, regarding psychopaths in organizations:

...psychopaths do work in modern organizations; they often are successful by most standard measures of career success; and their destructive personality characteristics are invisible to most of the people with whom they interact. They are able to circumvent and sometimes hijack succession planning and performance management systems in order to give legitimacy to their behaviors. They take advantage of communication weaknesses, organizational systems and processes, interpersonal conflicts, and general stressors that plague all companies.[81]

And another study, this time of British senior managers and executives, concluded (as reported by Babiak and Hare) that:

...the prevalence of histrionic, narcissistic, and compulsive personality disorders was relatively high, and that many of the traits exhibited were consistent with psychopathy: superficial charm, insincerity, egocentricity, manipulativeness, grandiosity, lack of empathy, exploitativeness, independence, rigidity, stubbornness, and dictatorial tendencies.

I would argue that this high preponderance of psychopathy among the ranks of senior business leaders, among zombie organizations, is not accidental. It is the direct result of the way operating systems within zombie organizations actually work. Such organizations select leaders who are egotistical, manipulative, lack empathy ("the bottom line!"), and dictatorial. Then, once those people are in power, they select others from that same mold.

They then spout slogans and doublespeak; some of their favorites include:

- "Rightsizing"

- "Do more with less"

- "Teamwork"

- "We need to transform."

Mindset/Engagement
Most people here are hoping to work somewhere else

There is an epidemic of disengagement in our workplaces. Gallup reports that, in 2015, only 32 percent of U.S. employees were "engaged," with the majority either (50.8 percent) "not engaged" or (17.2 percent) "actively disengaged." Over the proceeding 15 years that Gallup has been tracking this metric, there has been no large year-over-year improvements in employee engagement, with it consistently averaging less than 33 percent.[82] By the way, in case you were thinking that workers outside of the U.S. might be happier (perhaps the French or Germans with their long vacations), you would be wrong. Worldwide, the percentage of engaged workers drops to 13 percent.[83]

It is interesting to note that there is one cohort of workers—traditionalists—where engagement is substantially higher at 42.2 percent. However, for any generation younger than that—from Baby Boomers on down—the pattern is consistent: Only one-third or slightly less is engaged.

	2014
Traditionalists	42.2%
Baby Boomers	32.7%
Generation X	32.2%
Millennials	28.9%

Table 1: U.S. employee engagement by generation - 2014[84]

Not surprisingly, since organizations are largely using Taylorist-Monocratic bureaucracy (zombie) organization operating systems, "workers" with more power and control—such as those in the "managers, executive, or officer" category—have somewhat higher engagement at 38.4 percent (2014); while those in the "professional" and "clerical or office workers" categories match the average level of engagement at a dismal 32.4 percent and 31.8 percent, respectively.[85]

So, what does it take—at least according to Gallup's survey—to become "engaged" at work? Is it more money? More status? More intellectual challenge? The definition that Gallup uses is that, to be engaged, a worker would feel that they have:

- An opportunity to do what they do best each day

- Someone at work who encourages their development

- A belief that their opinions count at work.

In zombie organizations, workers feel they do NOT have opportunities to do what they do best every day; that NO ONE at work encourages their development; and they believe their opinions DO NOT count. To me it seems obvious that these perceptions follow naturally as a result of the zombie organizations' Taylorist perspective of workers, who, as you recall, are expected to just "do" their jobs. In this operating system, the opinions of workers are not as relevant as those of the all-knowing manager holding a stopwatch, with an organizational "best practice" for the worker to use.

Is it little wonder that LinkedIn is full of people all seemingly hoping that a recruiter will magically find them and transport them to a dream job? By one survey, 42 percent of managers in the United States are currently looking for a job at another organization—the same or roughly the same proportion of all employees who are Gen Y (42 percent) and Gen X (38 percent). Even the Baby Boomer generation, which reports the lowest level of job-seeking activity (perhaps reflecting their seniority in organizations and therefore higher switching costs), still has one in five people currently looking for a new job.[86]

Mindset/Engagement
We infrequently learn from our mistakes

Another critical part of an organization's mindset is an interest in and openness to learning. Organizations, in a fast-changing world, need to be adept at learning which predictions are working (and which are not), and using that information to update the model(s) the organization uses to make those decisions.

The best way for us to learn the most compelling lessons comes from receiving some sort of immediate negative feedback from something we did (i.e., we thought that it would work, but it didn't). Based on studies of brains in use, one typical way the brain can react is to treat the negative feedback as a stimulus for problem-solving—something our brains were evolved to do.[87] Neuroscientist Daniel Bor in his book, *The Ravenous Brain*, describes that a key component of our very consciousness is "the discovery of deep patterns within the contents of our awareness."[88] Our brains are wired to try to figure out what happened and why; and the brain increases its attention during the next decision. As it does, we get better at making these kinds of decisions (predictions) and our performance improves. This is the kind of reaction you would want at both an individual and organizational level.[89]

But the other, typical, way for the brain to react is to see this feedback as a threat. To escape feeling bad (following the SCARF model, the brain could see, for example, the possibility of reduced status or less certainty), the brain chooses not to think about the mistake. The brains of these people tend to pay much more attention whenever they receive positive feedback—evidence, the researchers thought, of confirmation bias.[90]

In zombie organizations, negative feedback (i.e., something didn't work) is seen as a "mistake"; and any mistake people make could be rating-reducing, or career-limiting, or worse. So individually and collectively, people avoid doing anything that could lead to a "mistake," and repeat anything that received a positive result (ignoring any contradictory information). The result is, of course, that nothing new is learned—either by simply not trying it, or by using confirmation bias to filter away any negative information.

Mindset/Engagement
People do not trust each other much here

Brené Brown, well-known "shame" researcher and speaker, said, "Vulnerability is the birthplace of innovation, creativity, and change."[91] It is very difficult to be vulnerable without trust; and without vulnerability, people can't learn; and, if people can't learn, organizations can't learn.

The word "trust" gets bandied around a lot, but what does it really mean within an organization? It is both a prediction and a bet. First, you predict, on the basis of incomplete information, that your colleague's behavior toward you is (1) based on positive intentions; and (2) competent and knowledgeable regarding the work or information you need. Second, you believe in your prediction sufficiently that you are willing to "bet" something on it; you could bet your status—by exposing your lack of knowledge to them by asking a question or making a suggestion; you could bet some future effort of yours—because, by asking them to do something for you now, you are creating a matching future obligation to do something for them later.

> "Trust can be more powerful than power. And it's vital for the collaboration that generates innovation and builds durable institutions."
>
> —Joel Peterson

Trust does matter to organizations. Joel Peterson, the chairman of Jet Blue and author of a recent book about trust, says, "Trust can be more powerful than power. And it's vital for the collaboration that generates innovation and builds durable institutions."[92] There is some significant scientific work to back up that claim: A meta-analysis of 119 academic articles covering 132 independent samples found these benefits for organizations:

- "The relationship between trust and job performance was as strong as or stronger than relationships with other attitudes such as job satisfaction"

- "Trust also predicted risk-taking, which is vital in many jobs where formal or legalistic controls do not protect exchange partners"

- "[Higher] trust also predicted [lower] counterproductive behaviors, which can prove quite costly to organizations even when the base rates for committing them remain low"

- "Trust was positively correlated with affective commitment, a significant predictor of both absenteeism and turnover"[93]

In short, trust is a critical variable that has a direct impact on the efficiency and effectiveness of organizations, and is a key source of competitive advantage.[94] Given its importance, it is frightening to find that only half of all employees (in organizations with 100 employees or more) say that they trust their senior management; and at the largest organizations (10,000+) it is only 43 percent.[95] And, as we have seen, the Taylorist approach makes the assumption that employees are untrustworthy, so controls and rules (and a bureaucracy to manage those) are required. The feeling, baked into a zombie organization's operating mindset, is mutual.

Communication
There are too many emails and other internal communications

Everyone complains about getting too many emails. They say it partly because they think it gives them status—as in, "Look how important I am that I get so many emails"; but it generally is true—people are actually overwhelmed.

According to one estimate, a typical worker received around 122 emails per day in 2015;[96] which, according to a study by Harris Interactive, is roughly two-and-a-half times more than what most employees thought they could handle.[97] Email eats up our time; according to a study by the McKinsey Global Institute, email consumes 28 percent of the average work week of "interaction workers."[98] And that time is largely wasted; another study, of a single company, estimated that only 20 percent of the time people were using email correctly—"to communicate across time zones or answer a well-defined question"—but the rest of the traffic was a waste.[99] And we know that people are checking their emails in meetings, at dinner with family or friends, and at bedtime—not the best for healthy social relations and a good night's sleep.

Communication

Part of the problem is that we are using email for everything:

- Communication

- To-do list

- Personal information management tool

- Information archive

- Collaboration with colleagues

- Assigning and delegating tasks[100]

Email itself is wasteful, but it is also distracting. One study found that employees were checking their email about once every two minutes (or 240 times/8-hour day);[101] by another study, people were checking it 74 times per day.[102] There is the time required to read and respond to the email—and then to file the email (and the reply). Then there is also the time required to restart the original, now interrupted, task. In one experiment, observing students writing a story on a computer who were interrupted for 30 seconds, it took them 10-15 seconds before they were back up to their original typing speed.[103]

Being interrupted and overwhelmed with messages is stressful. The combination has actually been shown to reduce workers' IQ: When monitoring the IQ of workers throughout the day, it was found that their IQ dropped by 10 points. That is the same as if they had missed a night of sleep, and considerably more than if they had smoked marijuana![104] Thierry Breton, CEO of Atos, an information technology company, calls email "pollution"—with only 20 useful emails out of the average 200 daily emails every one of his 76,000 employees received every day. His answer—email is banned for internal company communications.

Communication
People do not know what is going on across our organization

Just as much as people in zombie organizations complain about too much email, they also—ironically—complain about not knowing what is going on within the organization. Regularly, people are surprised to find out about some year-old project, or an org change in another part of the organization, or some strategic imperative they were previously unaware of.

Now, to be fair, they might have been sent an email about it, but that one got lost in the inbox deluge. Or it could have been that they were not on the right distribution list. Email takes silos to a whole new level with all information existing within the silo created by the "To" and "CC" lists; if you are not on those then you won't be told. Alternatively, organizations distribute information in meetings; but, again, you would have to be on the invitation list (and have the free time on your calendar to go to it, without checking your emails during the meeting).

What is the most important thing for the staff in any organization to know? The business strategy. Giam Swiegers, CEO of Deloitte Australia, says this about the importance of communicating an organization's strategy: "At the end of the day, every executive wakes up in the morning and says, 'I have a good strategy, how do I get people to execute it?'"[105] He goes on to tell the story of debating a first-year associate who had challenged Swiegers' diversity strategy in a firm-wide discussion forum.

This story is so shocking because, in the zombie organizations we are used to, there is no real way for the "bottom" to communicate with the "top," and to then have a dialogue around important questions like what the strategy is, whether it is working or not, and what the organization could do better.

Communication
It's hard for someone to get useful feedback on their ideas

When someone says, "I have an idea that we should do 'X,'" what they are really saying is, "I have an idea that if we do 'X'—this new thing—then I predict we will get 'Y' desirable outcome." In a VUCA-digital world, we will need lots of good "ideas" like this.

Proposing these new predictions is really about creating new knowledge, and adding or enhancing or changing the model of the world that the organization uses to guide its activities. Having "good" ideas requires getting feedback—lots and lots of feedback, especially from those within (although not exclusively within) your organization. Yet, few of us have been trained to give or receive feedback effectively. For feedback to do its job, we need to be able to understand it, accept it, and know what to do with it. Getting there is both science and art.[106]

It is a delicate thing to bring an idea forward—risking that you will be seen as your organization's "village idiot"; and it is a challenging thing to encourage that vulnerability while providing a useful critique of the idea and its merits. Zombie organizations simply don't have the mechanisms for providing feedback. The culture is antithetical to the kind of vulnerability required, and people working in the organizations don't have the skills or models for doing so.

Collaboration/Decision-making
Coordinating work with people in other parts of the organization is hard

Organizations need to coordinate the work that people are doing, across geographies, across functional groups, and across customer/client groups (e.g., by industry or market segment). In zombie organizations, this is hard to do. The result is the classic uncoordinated hand-foot jerking, slow, stumbling run, and tendency not to get out of the way of moving vehicles.

Why is it so hard for the left hand to know what the right hand is doing in a zombie organization? The root cause is that, using Taylor's model from the industrial age, the base and generally unfounded assumption is that people's work is both compartmentalized and visible. This makes sense when you are building car parts—each worker does his or her own function and passes it on to the next; and you can see—looking across the factory floor—who is doing what work, and what state it is in (the weld made, the parts assembled, the forms shuffled from in-basket to out-basket).

But nowadays, as we have discussed earlier, most of that work has been either automated, offshored, or outsourced. The remaining, nonroutine work (of making predictions and bets in a VUCA-digital world) is, by definition, neither compartmentalized nor visible. You can't see into a product designer's mind to see what she is working on; you can't tell whether she is typing up some product specifications or updating her LinkedIn résumé. And someone in Marketing (who would want to know about new products), or someone in Operations (who has to build it), or someone in Procurement (who has to source the parts)...can't see the work on that new product, or see how it might fit into their work.

Most of the work in today's organization is like dark matter and energy in the universe: We know it is there, and we know it makes up most of what the organization does (95 percent when it comes to dark matter and energy in the universe),[107] but we just can't see it. Dark matter is defined as "nonluminous material" sitting in the dark—just try coordinating an organization full of that!

Smart organizations know how to make that work visible—staff within an organization can see how their work fits with others' so that collision points are reduced or eliminated, reinventing the wheel is a thing of the past, and the sum of the whole becomes greater than the sum of the parts.

Of course, organizations also need to coordinate work with close outsiders, like suppliers, partners, technology vendors, and alumni or other "friends" of the organizations. Likely there will be more, not fewer, of these "inside outsiders," as organizations move to on-demand models for certain work and partnerships to extend an organization's reach and capabilities without incurring additional costs. This problem of coordination, which is already bad, is just going to get worse.

Collaboration/Decision-making
It is easy to get to a "No" decision, and hard to get a "Yes"

One characteristic of zombie organizations is that there are many decision-making paths to take you to a "no"; and few, or zero, paths to get a "yes." "You can't," "it's not permitted," "so-and-so won't like that," and "you'll have to check with the 'X' department" are a few of the oft-heard responses to proposals.

In one study, an aerospace company needed to make a single change to a contract. The approval process involved 125 different

ORGANIZATIONAL COMPLEXITY AT AN AEROSPACE COMPANY

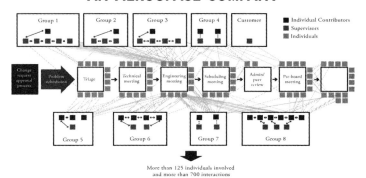

Figure 13: Making one change to a contract[108]

> "Getting a decision to try something new becomes akin to running a marathon, through the Hogwart's Triwizard Maze, in the middle of the Hunger Games."

people and more than 700 interactions. How many opportunities for "no" were there in that process?

And just try to do something novel in a zombie organization; it is exhausting and career limiting (since changing something invariably is goring someone's ox). Getting a decision to try something new becomes akin to running a marathon, through the Hogwart's Triwizard Maze, in the middle of the Hunger Games.

Collaboration/Decision-making
Meetings here are useless and unproductive

Meetings, whether face-to-face or digital, can help speed the resolution of an issue or get faster, better decisions made. However, in zombie organizations, such success is generally the exception to the rule. Meetings in organizations with a high "Z" score tend to be longer, unfocused, and with unnecessary people in attendance. Sometimes there are pre-meetings for certain participants to plan what they are going to do, or not do, at the meeting. Ernst & Young executive Al Pittampalli says they are "not about coordination, but about a bureaucratic excuse-making and the kabuki dance of company politics."[109]

Of course, if everyone can say no, and people work in silos, and the world keeps changing, and no one really reads their emails carefully (because they are overwhelmed and interrupted), you need lots of meetings just to keep the wheels of the organization churning. One study says executives spend 40-50 percent of their total working hours in meetings—with almost 34 percent of all meetings ending up as wasted time. That means executives are basically wasting a day every week. By one estimate, this wasted meeting time means a loss of productivity valued at nearly $47 billion just in the United States.[110]

Unfortunately, it is not just a problem of wasted time. In zombie organizations, already suffering from reduced diversity, meetings engender groupthink. Symptoms of groupthink include:

- Collective rationalization—where members do not reconsider their assumptions, and discount alternative views

- Self-censorship—people with doubts about the perceived group consensus don't express them

- Illusion of unanimity—where the majority's judgment or perspective is assumed to be held by everyone in the group[111]

How many projects went on to their doom as the result of groupthink taking over, enhanced and enforced in meetings? How many opportunities to make a better product, or provide a better service, or to future-proof the organization, were wasted by meeting groupthink?

In the next set of chapters, we will look at each Mindset/Engagement, Communication, and Collaboration/Decision-making in more detail, and what the system components of a "smart" operating system would look like.

CHAPTER 5
Mindset and match: The way zombie organizations think and how to change them

Our brains become magnetized with the dominating thoughts which we hold in our minds, and...these "magnets" attract to us the forces, the people, the circumstances of life, which harmonize with the nature of our dominating thoughts.

—Napoleon Hill[112]

An engaged staff and an "open" mindset—these are the hallmarks of a smart organization. Zombie organizations, in contrast, have disengaged employees and a "closed" culture (or what Carol Dweck, in her book *Mindset*, called a "fixed" mindset).

Before I take you through what an organizational mindset might be, and why it matters, and the difference between an "open" and "closed" one, it would be useful to remind ourselves of the most important work for an organization. In a VUCA-digital world, the most important work of an organization is to make predictions, based on limited and imperfect information, about what is going to happen—and then to place a "bet" (or not) on that outcome.

Making predictions in a VUCA-digital world, perforce, is difficult because nothing stays the same, everything is connected to everything else, and there is a lot of noise in the information where the signal (the truth!) is hiding. Smart organizations handle this problem in two ways fundamentally different from zombie ones:

- All hands on deck: Smart organizations have everyone in the organization scouting for, and filtering, information about what is going on (or not going on)

- Learning imperative: The organization actively tries to learn as much as possible about what seems to be important right now (and be willing to abandon what had been learned for something new that "works" better—i.e., explains better what is going on)

Zombie organizations take a quite different approach:

- Poop deck is tops: Zombie organizations focus the scouting for, and filtering of, information in the hands of a few—either specialized units (e.g., market research, business intelligence) or the senior leadership

- Learning reluctance: The organizations are willing to learn, but only if that learning does not undermine the existing status quo, both political (i.e., the current leadership) or financial (i.e., the current business model)

By one estimate, two-thirds of strategic intelligence for an organization comes from information sources and human networks. So, part of the success of smart organizations comes purely from a numbers game: A smart organization, with 1,000 people part-time scouting for information, clearly is going to do better than 10 or 20 or 30 doing so.

Having so many people scouting is obviously better, but, according to Professor Jeong-Nam Kim from Purdue University, it is not just the volume of information but the quality as well:

> To a certain extent all employees are trained experts in their respective area of corporate business function or process. A major portion of their job activities is to initiate and maintain informal and formal communicative interactions with consumers, government regulatory agencies, partners, and suppliers. These key publics and stakeholders are the main sources of begetting new opportunities (e.g., new product ideas, creation of niche market) and impending threats (e.g., hostile regulation, market failing). Therefore, each and every employee is in the frontline of potential information mines, detecting what is going in and around their organization and anticipating future needs.[113]

Smart organizations combine this all-hands scouting activity with a drive to learn. This drive includes an understanding that, in a VUCA-digital world, many bets made on predictions from within the organization will not turn out to be true (or will only be partly true and, therefore, only partly pay off). These are not career-limiting "failures"; and the organization is not suffused with the sense that Damocles' sword—of blame—hangs over them. In a smart organization, the bets that don't pay off—as long as they were made with care and consideration—are treated as an opportunity to learn a lesson (albeit a painful one).

Making an effort, facing challenges, experiencing setbacks, not getting it right the first time—these are all expected by leaders in a smart organization. If it was that easy to know exactly what to do (e.g., which functions to add, what technology to buy, which markets to enter or leave, what changes in processes should be made), then everyone would already have done them (or be in the process of doing them), so any value to the organization would be quickly lost. The effort and struggle actually reflect that learning is happening; and that learning leads to sustaining change.

Another thing that happens in smart organizations—beyond having everyone participate with the drive for learning—is that groupthink is avoided. Here's how Dweck compares two groups: one with a fixed mindset and the other with a growth mindset:

> ...as time went on the growth-mindset groups clearly outperformed the fixed-mindset ones. And this difference became ever larger the longer the groups worked. Once again, those with the growth mindset profited from their mistakes and feedback far more than the fixed-mindset people. But what was even more interesting was how the groups functioned. The members of the growth-mindset groups were much more likely to state their honest opinions and openly express their disagreements as they communicated about their management decisions. Everyone was part of the learning process. For the fixed-mindset groups—with their concern about who was smart or dumb or their anxiety about disapproval for their ideas—that open, productive discussion did not happen. Instead, it was more like groupthink.[114]

If you work in a zombie organization, you probably recognize the "fixed" or "closed" mindset at play:

- There is always a desire to look smart—in the eyes of the customers, the stock market, prospective hires

- Significant challenges are to be avoided—preferably by not deciding anything and putting off doing anything until absolutely necessary

- There is little or no effort put into trying something new (ironically, a zombie organization will spend an enormous amount of effort doing it the old way, but little to try a new way that might be less work)

- Negative feedback is experienced as criticism—with the source either denigrated or ignored

To be clear, there is a danger of anyone with significant experience and training developing, if not a "fixed" view, then at least a resistant one. This disease—expertise-itis—occurs when, as Harold Laski, a 20th century political theorist put it: "Expertise... breeds an inability to accept new views from the very depths of its preoccupation with its own conclusions." In essence, those who suffer from expertise-itis stop receiving feedback because their previous success triggers confirmation bias. "Their interpretations of data are akin to the cliché of the butcher putting his thumb on the scale. They know what they want to find, and lo and behold, they find it!"[116]

In zombie organizations, expertise-itis runs rampant, with the entire organization turned into a row of butchers, each with

"Expertise...breeds an inability to accept new views from the very depths of its preoccupation with its own conclusions."

—Harold Laski[115]

his thumb on the scale for which he is responsible. SMART goal performance systems encourage them to stay in line, and to continue to produce insights in line with those they produced last year (no matter what has changed). Everything around them, rooted in the organization's culture, encourages them to toe the line and not ask too many questions.

Organizational or company culture is an increasingly hot topic—the number of Google searches on the term "company culture" has roughly doubled over the last 10 years[117] and you can get almost seven million hits for the term. Culture can be a slippery and abstract word. A useful definition is offered by Sara Roberts in her book *Nimble, Focused, Feisty*:

> ...the set of tacit understandings and beliefs that drive behaviors, ways of thinking, and ways of talking and interacting that the people within a particular group perceive are right or normal. These, in turn, shape the practices of the group, the outputs of its work, and its reputation or brand. In other words, I see culture most tangibly in how people act, including how they make decisions, how they treat colleagues and customers, how they define and reward success, talk about problems, view the world, plan for the future, develop products, etc.[118]

An organization's culture builds up over time—reinforced by the successes (and failures) it experiences. Zombie organizations have "suffered" from too much success for too long using their current operating system. There is a reinforcing effect where our social brains form a view of the world based the feedback they are receiving; but what the brain sees, and how it interprets it, is mediated by its social situation. And that social situation is dominated by the others in that zombie organization—all of whom share that same worldview! Our social brains—sitting in the dark and surrounded by bone—sense, and make-sense in a strange loop; in this loop, sensing leads to sense-making (within a social context) which, in turn, leads back to sensing.[119]

The result is a "locked-in" view of the world, and a locked-in way of behaving and thinking. While it is no longer true that you can tell by how someone dresses whether they work at IBM or not, it is true that "locked-in" thinking is alive and well. For example, it seems incredible now to think about it, but Blockbuster once had upstart Netflix almost knocked down, and was moving into a digital future. At the time, in 2007, the Blockbuster board of directors brought in a new CEO from 7-Eleven who said: "The Internet is worthless, and we're getting out of it." His answer was an entertainment convenience store.[120] I wonder how that turned out?

A smart organization does three things differently from a zombie one; and these three things help drive the mindset, which, in turn, reinforces its actions so that a virtuous—or smart—circle is formed.

First, it uses zero-based thinking (ZBT). Like zero-based budgeting, where everyone's budget is reset to zero for every budget cycle, ZBT says:[121]

- Everything an organization is doing today can be changed or stopped (they were bets made, based on a prediction that made sense at one time, that did pay off, but might not be paying off any longer)

- Each of those bets—on an activity or project or investment or structure—has an opportunity cost (we could bet our time/money/effort on something else)

- That opportunity cost should be evaluated relative to:

  o The degree to which those bets make the organization comparatively better to whatever alternatives exist or are likely to exist

  o Finding the 20 percent of effort to deliver 80 percent of value (Pareto principle)

- Sunk costs are sunk—let them go

The implications of ZBT are potentially enormous; it suggests that organizations ask themselves questions like: Is this current customer of ours worth having? Is there a new technology that would be better? Why do we think our current business model still makes sense? What new opportunities exist for us? We are 50 percent more efficient now—what more can we do? These questions drive continual improvement—both incremental and transformative. They encourage prototyping and testing (it is low effort/cost to create a low-fidelity test to examine a new proposal). And they encourage diversity—since the more perspectives you can have on your business, the better.

But ZBT won't work with a top-down, siloed, blame-game-based organizational culture. You can see that culture all around you. It is in the physical organization of the workplace (there is a reason they are called cubicles—the organization literally wants people to work in a box). You can see it in the communication system (email or phones) that only allows point-to-point communication so a few can talk with a few, with the few-to-many communications reserved for the almighty leaders. You see it in the seemingly arbitrarily selected few "high performers," who receive the lion's share of the spoils (with the leaders typically raking in their big salaries and big bonuses).

And you see it in the new "transformation" initiatives, announced at zombie organizations with great fanfare and visionary titles. These initiatives, according to the Boston Consulting Group, "are often mere euphemisms for cost reduction" and don't deliver—75 percent of the time—the promised enhanced competitiveness and growth.[122] You can see in Figure 14 how, after one year, only 25 percent of these efforts show longer-term growth (the shaded box).

Basically, these "transformations" have the same track record as a fad diet: much ballyhooed as the latest thing, much pain and effort to go through them, and yet—a year later—the dieter is back to his/her old weight (or worse) again.

You can see the zombie culture in the metaphors that organizational leaders use in their messaging: winners and losers;

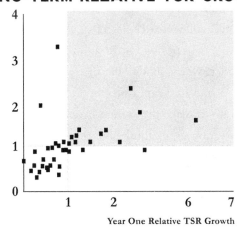

Source: GCG Analysis
Note: Based on a representative analysis of 48 companies publicly undergoing corporate transformation efforts. Total shareholder return (TSR) is adjusted by S&P 500 growth; 1=same growth rate as the index. Long-term growth refers to a period of five years or a period that is ongoing (that is, transformations begun since July 2008).

Figure 14: Transformation efforts usually fail - BCG[123]

wars and battles; "corrective action." And you see it more in their actions, highlighting the disconnect between what they say and what they actually care about. Is it little wonder that staff read announcements by the organization's leadership as if they were the latest edition of Pravda? Employees notice the wide gap between the stated intent—"This is a vitally important new initiative" vs. the actual investment (i.e., the amount of time and effort the leader actually puts into it). This corrosive gap between reality and pronouncements explains why Dilbert is so popular.

Leaders in smart organizations ensure that, through their behavior and their actions, they shape the organization's culture. Remember the SCARF model? Leaders at smart organizations try to make people feel safe, not by saying "ask me anything," but by demonstrating that it is actually career-enhancing (Status!) to ask hard questions about what the leadership is thinking or doing. They work hard at making sure there is transparency—so that staff aren't surprised (Certainty!) and can see that things are fair (Fairness!). Leaders in smart organizations think of ways to make their people feel connected (Related!) to those they work with, and that is more than paying for the annual holiday party.

These leaders worry about what the mindset (culture) of the organization is, and try to measure how it is changing, and what they need to do to make the culture better support trust, learning, and innovation. They think about symbols and how things might be perceived and interpreted (e.g., executives can fly first class, but everyone else is in coach). They look at internal processes such as the budget cycle (is it rear-facing and cost-focused, or future-oriented and value-focused?) or expense approvals (do they encourage responsible behavior or "find the loophole in the rule"?) to see what culture these factors drive. And they think a lot about who joins the organization and how those people will contribute to the organization's culture (and they are on the lookout for any psychopaths who might have managed to slip in, so they can expel them quickly).

Another thing smart organizations do is to recognize that the purpose of making money—either individually or collectively as an organization—is certainly necessary, although insufficient. Smart organizations provide employees a reason beyond their paycheck. Simon Sinek, who popularized the need to understand the importance of an organization's "why," explained it this way: "Working hard for something we don't care about is called stress; working hard for something we love is called passion."[124] Giving people a purpose that they can be passionate about means the organization can tap into the reservoirs of additional effort that staff can put into work; by reducing the stress (because people are doing what they want to do, rather than what they have to do), they free up more energy; and, by having a shared purpose, they engender trust across the organization since everyone within the organization shares the same goal.

But can a law firm, for example, have a higher purpose than making (mostly) white, middle-aged guys wealthier? It can. One employment law firm says its purpose is that "everyone is different...And any system that tries to treat us all as exactly the same is flawed and demeaning."[125] The "why" of an organization resonates with clients/customers, with potential hires, and with

"Working hard for something we don't care about is called stress; working hard for something we love is called passion."

—Simon Sinek

potential business partners. It attracts them to the organization; and it helps align people together. In smart organizations, purpose releases extra energy and gives context for everyone's regular work and "scouting" activities. Deloitte reports that organizations with a strong sense of purpose are significantly more confident their organizations will grow (82 percent versus 48 percent), and are optimistic that they will outperform their competitors long term (79 percent versus 7 percent).[126]

In smart organizations, workers have a genuine attachment to the organization and are intrinsically aligned with purpose. The leaders have a positive view of the people who work there—and that feeling is reciprocated. There is intrinsic motivation; and peer pressure works to help ensure alignment with the goals of the organization. Diversity—in hiring, in promotions, in participation—is not a "must-comply" requirement, but, instead, a prized part of how the organization can be successful. Mindsets are open, and feedback—up, down, inside, outside—is sought-after and used.

CHAPTER 6

Fast-flow communications: Why zombies can't walk and chew gum at the same time

Everything that moves, whether animate or inanimate, is a flow system. All flow systems generate shape and structure in time in order to facilitate this movement across a landscape filled with resistance (for example, friction)...Flow systems have two basic features (properties). There is the current that is flowing (for example...information) and the design through which it flows.

—Professor Adrian Bejan, *Design in Nature*[127]

Zombies, traditionally, don't think very quickly and have uncoordinated movements. The same can be said of zombie organizations. Even an organization with an open mindset, where people within the organization are focused on learning and aligned with a purpose, will have trouble responding quickly to the environment and coordinating activities. This is because the flow of information (like what-is-going-on scouting information) and the flow of ideas (How should we change how we think the world works? Or what should we do about it?) is simply not fast enough.

The first problem for zombie organizations is that they rely on what they already know (e.g., "brains are good") and look to incrementally increase their information about that. Smart organizations, in contrast, keep working away at what is not known— and keep a suspicious eye on what is already "known." Former U.S. Secretary of Defense Donald Rumsfeld famously provided an excellent set of categories for states of "knowing" during a news briefing on the evidence (or, rather, lack thereof) of weapons of mass destruction allegedly held by the Iraqi government at the time:

> ...we know, there are known knowns; there are things we know we know. We also know there are known unknowns; that is to say, we know there are some things we do not know. But there are also unknown unknowns— the ones we don't know we don't know. And...it is the latter category that tend to be the difficult ones.[128]

Smart organizations know that the unknown unknowns are the difficult ones—difficult both to understand, and difficult in that they cause difficulties. Smart organizations are constantly trying, therefore, to shift them into at least the "known unknown" category. They equally know that the "knowns" may not remain that way, and are always looking for signals (in the noise) that what they have been doing isn't working anymore (or won't work in the future).

One way to describe this is what KM-thought leader Karl Wiig called "situation handling" (see Figure 15) whereby an initial situation occurs (e.g., sales for a product increase), and the person or team or organization first goes through "sense-making" to build an understanding of the situation. With the situation understood (model making), the organization moves into decision-making or problem-solving (prediction making), and from there into the execution of whatever action is to be taken, if any (the laying of the bet). In doing so, the organization makes use of mental models as to how the world works.

SITUATION HANDLING
REQUIRES KNOWLEDGE

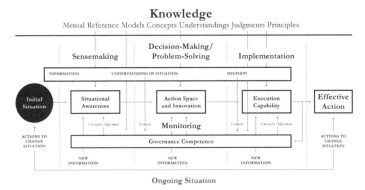

Figure 15: Karl Wiig's Situation Handling model[129]

Following the action, the cycle is repeated: Sense-making occurs to see how the prediction/bet is paying off—now based on more information from both the first sense-making, and whatever resulted from the action.

Smart organizations go beyond simply responding to situations—they also test how accurate their current model(s) are by probing the world around them. Some team or group within the organization has an idea about what the organization might do to its advantage; they try it—and see what happens. They do this, as much as possible, by devising low-fidelity prototypes and using them in low-risk ways (e.g., trying a new web page structure for a limited time with a subset of website visitors). Why this approach? Organizational social media expert and author Euan

Semple provides the answer: "I was once offered a Scotsman's tip on ROI—keep the 'I' really small and no one will give you hassle about the 'R.'"[130]

Smart organizations work to ensure that, at every level of the organization, this process is happening again, and again, in an automatic and nearly organic way. This or similar processes go by other names such as the Plan-Do-Check-Act (PDCA) cycle[131] or the Experiential Learning cycle. What is important to understand is that the cycle, when working well, is constantly improving the sophistication of the person, the team, or the organization's understanding of what is going on in one particular situation, while also contributing to the understanding of other situations and circumstances.

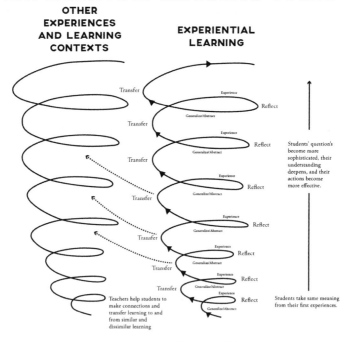

Figure 16: Experiential learning spiral[132]

This process of situation handling with PDCA, and sharing those learnings in other contexts, works to constantly, gradually, reduce the unknown unknowns. This protects the organization from the VUCA-digital world.

Smart organizations need "fast-flow" communications of information and ideas between all the people in the organization, and between the outside of the organization and the inside, so that the organization's predictions and bets can get better. With the external environment changing so quickly, and with the internal organizing making new predictions with different kinds of bets, it is imperative that the people in the organization have access to all kinds of information related to the various situations they are facing (or opportunities they are testing).

That information is typically new, emerging from what is going on now; it provides feedback on how previous similar actions (predictions and bets) have worked. Smart organizations also need access to their colleagues' mental models and ideas: models as to how the world works now and how it might work in the future, and ideas for things to try (i.e., new predictions with new bets) to improve the organization in some way. To do this efficiently and effectively, smart organizations use communication platforms that are designed to be "open," "pull," and with "context." "Open"—so everyone can access everything (within legal or proprietary limits); "pull"—so that employees can assemble what they need, when they need it (rather than have information pushed to them based on the sender's timetable); and with "context"—so the puller can better process the information (i.e., context as to which project or piece of work, who is the author, what preceded in the conversation).

Zombie organizations have need of "what is going on" and "what do you think might happen if..." information-sharing as

> "Zombie organizations have need of 'what is going on' and 'what do you think might happen if...' information-sharing as well. However, they use an outmoded communications platform using a format and thinking that dates back to the early 20th century."

well. However, they use an outmoded communications platform using a format and thinking that dates back to the early 20th century. As a result, managers in organizations spend up to two hours per day searching for information—and more than 50 percent of the information they obtain has no value to them. Nearly three out of five respondents (59 percent) in one survey said that, as a consequence of poor information distribution, they miss information that might be valuable to their jobs almost every day (e.g., the information does exist somewhere else in the company, but they just cannot find it). And it is not just wasted time and effort; 42 percent of respondents said they accidentally use wrong information at least once a week. What is the cost and risk of that to zombie organizations?[133]

What is this platform? It is email, which, as a technology, dates back to the 1970s; but as a format of communication, a closed-push model, it goes back 50 more years. Here's an example (see Figure 17) from the Smithsonian of a memo from 1918. Notice the classic "To," "From," and "Subject" structure, which is instantly recognizable from the 100-plus emails you probably received today.

The memo (email) is pushed by the sender to the receiver(s), is only available to those it was sent to (closed)—and therefore realistically only sent to a few people (sending an email to "All staff" is typically unavailable to the average corporate citizen, and

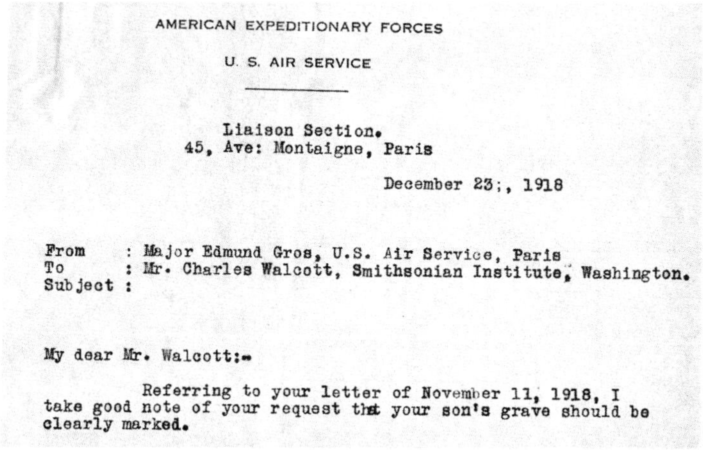

AMERICAN EXPEDITIONARY FORCES

U. S. AIR SERVICE

Liaison Section.
45, Ave: Montaigne, Paris

December 23;, 1918

From : Major Edmund Gros, U.S. Air Service, Paris
To : Mr. Charles Walcott, Smithsonian Institute, Washington.
Subject :

My dear Mr. Walcott:-

Referring to your letter of November 11, 1918, I take good note of your request that your son's grave should be clearly marked.

Figure 17: Example of a memo with "From," "To," and "Subject" headings[134]

is reserved for pronouncements by the leaders). Beyond the title/date of the email, there is precious little context to assist the receiver in knowing what (if anything) to do with the information (i.e., What is this email related to? Are there other questions that are involved? Who else has been involved in the discussion to-date? And who are those people?).

Email has other problems as well: It is designed to interrupt the receiver. You must look at it to know if you need to look at it. Once you take action, email requires both the sender and receiver to figure out some way to file the email—either for future reference or in the wastebasket (and, of course, filing the reply, if any). Now you have multiple copies stored in different places under different categories. Of course, the email is also not available to anyone else who did not receive it originally (new team members, for example, that join a project team later). Finally, it was not designed for conversation; when you reply, the system simply appends the entire previous "memo" underneath your new one.

The alternative communication platforms that smart companies use—like team-chat-based Slack, or enterprise-social-net-

> "The key difference between the two systems is that, in email, every piece of content (an email itself) goes separately to, and is held privately by, every person it is addressed to; whereas in a 'fast-flow' communication platform, the content is simply available to everyone at any time (although an individual may be specifically notified when content addressed to them is newly available)."

working Jive—are designed to be "pull" based so that employees can get what they need, when they need it. Employees do that by going to the project space, topic, or group that is relevant to their current work to get up to speed on the questions and issues and ideas (based on their timing and not the timing of when the questions or issues or ideas were shared). These systems are "open," and operate on a many-to-many basis so that everyone (with appropriate access) can pull to them what they need (since you can never predict, in a VUCA-digital world, what topic or piece of information is related to any other topic or piece of information). And the information has context: The person's name who posted something relevant to you is linked to their profile showing who they are and what else they have posted; the previous conversation is available along with the latest post; links to documents go to the current version (not the version that was originally attached, as you have in emails).

The key difference between the two systems is that, in email, every piece of content (an email itself) goes separately to, and is held privately by, every person it is addressed to; whereas in a "fast-flow" communication platform, the content is simply available to everyone at any time (although an individual may be specifically notified when content addressed to them is newly available). This many-to-many approach—see Figure 18—(in contrast to email's few-to-few approach) means that people are not interrupted by things arriving, but can retrieve them when they need them for their work. It means that the content survives and is useful long after that original conversation took place (e.g., someone joining six months after a conversation can discover the content of the conversation, who the participants were, and the background of those participants).

ONE-TO-MANY VS. MANY-TO-MANY COMMUNICATIONS

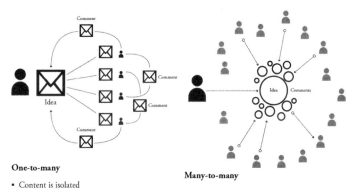

One-to-many

- Content is isolated
- Limited to people who received the message
- Disappears over time
- Email groups must be constantly managed

Many-to-many

- Content is persistent
- Available from anywhere, to everyone, at any time
- Groups are created organically by following

Figure 18: Content is openly available to be pulled when needed[135]

So why is this open-pull-context system so much better than the closed-push-no-context system? To understand this, you first must think about information and ideas moving through an organization as a flow system. Like water trickling or rushing downhill, information flows from the originator of the information or idea (which is, after all, just information itself) to others within the organization. Professor Adrian Bejan has developed an understanding of how that flow works:

Like any other point-area flow in nature, a new idea spreads on the landscape in two ways, via two flow mechanisms:

1. Fast, along pre-existing (established) channels of prior interest in what spreads, and

2. Slow, perpendicularly to the lines, sweeping the interstices that fill the landscape.[136]

Email, because the sender sends to only those they think would be interested, acts to follow the "pre-existing (established) channels of prior interest." That is, email supports the transmittal of ideas or information that is congruent with the organization's current model of the world as accepted by the hierarchical powers-that-be (the most obvious example would be an email from the CEO to everyone telling them something). Novel ideas (i.e., those that are not congruent with the current model) diffuse slowly through the "interstices," more likely through one-on-one conversations (in person or in email).

Bejan explains that "flow systems have two basic features (properties)...the current that is flowing (for example...information) and the design through which it flows."[137] The "secret sauce" of the smart organization's open-pull-context communication systems is that it changes the design through which information flows; now anyone in the organization—from any geography or functional group or level in the hierarchy—can find any prior conversation or file or work task that is relevant to them and join in (or start a new one). Like removing dams and channels so a river can diffuse into the sea more easily, this new communications platform dramatically reduces the friction for a new idea or new information to spread through the organization. The consulting company McKinsey estimates that improving communication and collaboration by such social technologies can improve the productivity of what they call "interaction workers" by 20-25 percent.[138] This is the reason for the astonishing growth—see Figure 19—of the various email alternatives (e.g., Slack, Hip-Chat, Asana) that are available today.

GROWTH OF SLACK, HIPCHAT, ASANA SOFTWARE

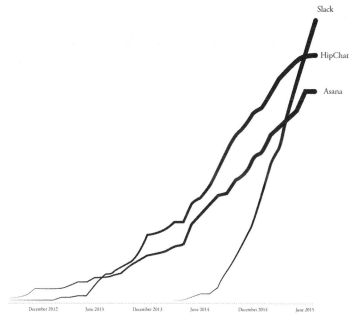

Figure 19: Explosive growth of open-pull communication systems[139]

Another flow blocker in an organization, aside from the way email works as a closed-push-no-context system, is that the work itself is typically hidden. Can you see a marketing analyst working on the latest sales figures? Can you tell if an IT strategist is actually strategizing? No, you can't. Unlike assembling a car, or serving hamburgers, or data entry, there is no "line of sight" on work that is nonroutine, collaborative, and creative—the bulk, and the most important part, of the work of organizations in a VUCA-digital world. Like the dark matter we spoke of earlier, we know it makes up the majority of the activity, but no one can see it.

And, because we can't see it, it is difficult for employees or managers to coordinate their work together. A significant part of any manager's time is spent trying to identify collision, intersection, or points for the projects and work they are responsible for; to dampen the worst impacts and, hopefully, find and exploit opportunities to reinforce work that connects with another team. It is difficult to coordinate and communicate outside of the organization—with clients/customers, with suppliers, with partners, with stakeholders—about the state of the work (i.e., what is to be done, what is being done now, what has been completed).

One result of this is to increase email traffic as staff and managers try to share or discover with others what work is being done by whom. Email becomes not just a tool for communication, but also a tool for managing and coordinating tasks. Here's how it works: I send you an email asking you to review a paragraph in a document I am preparing. I keep a copy of that email so I can remember who and when I asked. After a couple of days, since you didn't reply, and because I am nervous about the timeline, I forward you the first email and ask that you confirm that you received the first email and have started the review. You now reply, saying that you have been slammed with work, but you will be free shortly and will complete your part by the end of the week. So, you have three emails to confirm (1) ownership of the work;

(2) current status; and (3) target completion date. We could explore this example further (What if the end of the week is too late? What if the review is out of the scope of expertise of the reviewer? What if some other work comes up and the reviewer is no longer available?), but won't.

One alternative that organizations have tried is some sort of task management tool. (Outlook has "Tasks" built in.) These invariably get little use, which is odd given the size of the problem. This lack of use is partly because the tasks largely exist, like emails, without much context—one task on a list of tasks looks much like another, even though one is larger or more important.[140] The list of tasks also isn't typically shared with others; and there is a lot of evidence to suggest that the public accountability created when you share a goal (a task is nothing other than a goal by another name) means you are much more likely to get it done as compared to a goal that wasn't shared.[141] Finally, lists of tasks are hard for us humans to "get." We like stories, and have an instinctual need for them.[142] As social psychologist Jonathan Haidt says: "The human mind is a story processor, not a logic processor"— and lists are all about logic and not stories.[143]

There is an alternative that smart organizations use—it is a visual management approach called kanban—that has its roots in the Toyota Way and "lean" thinking. Instead of having lists, you have cards (one for each piece of work), arranged in columns on a board. The titles of the column reflect the state of the work; in the simplest arrangement, these would be familiar to anyone who

> "The human mind is a story processor, not a logic processor."
>
> —Jonathan Haidt

uses a notebook or task list to track their own work: "To Do," "Doing," and "Done." The boards provide public accountability and tell a story ("Wow! We've done a lot of work"; or "Oh, no! There is a lot of work to do"). See Figure 20 to see what a simple board would look like.

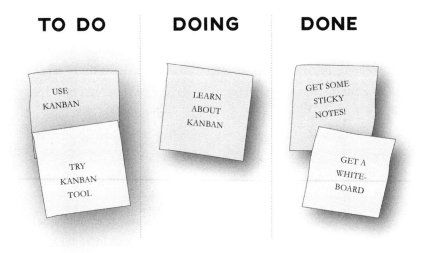

TO DO   DOING   DONE

Figure 20: Simple kanban board[144]

The simplicity of the approach belies the profound difference that results from the vastly increased flow of information about the work both within a team and across teams (and, indeed, at an enterprise level when the boards are digitally available). Who is doing what (both at the team and individual level) is now available to anyone with access to the boards; of course, the default for access ought to be "open" so that anyone in the organization can "pull," from any of the boards, what they need (when they need it), and who is doing what. At a team level, and at an inter-team level, staff and managers can now see intersections with other teams.

For example, if a team purchasing a new IT system needs a security review of a possible software, they could add that to the "Intake" column of the IT Security team's "Reviews" board. The card with the work on it can contain due dates, size estimates, checklists, priority levels, etc. And the project team can see progress on their review as it is first moved into the "To Do" column (i.e., the IT Security team has taken on the work) and see as it is assigned to one of the IT Security team members (i.e., who is going to do the work). Then they can see as it is moved, by that member, into the "Doing" column (so they know the work has been started). And, finally, they can see as the work is completed when it is moved into the "Done" column.

Organizing tasks in boards gives a visual representation of the work that is readable at a glance (e.g., if there are a lot of cards in the "To Do" column, then there is a lot of work that hasn't been started yet). It gives teams, and teams of teams, the opportunity to look at the work and have extremely productive meetings to better organize, reprioritize, and restructure the work so that it flows faster and more efficiently. Boards nested within other boards can enable a portfolio management approach to the work, which is essentially how, in reality, work is organized. But with such poor information about the state of work, it can take days, weeks, or even months for a change in one area to cascade over to another affected work team.

The combination of open-pull-context communication—with open-pull-context work structure (in kanban boards) reduces the information (and idea) friction within smart organizations so they can more quickly learn, share what they are learning, and make consequent changes in their organization. Having one—improved communication—or the other—improved work coordination—of course, has value. But the combination of the two together is extraordinarily powerful. At the end of the day, it is not just about information or work coordination for organizations; it is most importantly about making and implementing decisions that make an organization truly smart.

CHAPTER 7
Accelerated decision-making:
Zombies have a one-track mind

*Ultimately, a company's value is no more (and no less) than
the sum of the decisions it makes and executes.*

—Marcia W. Blenko, Michael C. Mankins, and Paul Rogers,
The Decision-Driven Organization[145]

You can have all the learning (from your open organizational
mindset), and you can have super-fast, open communication
of information, but, unless your organization decides—and then
does something—your organization won't be much better than
the zombies.

To be fair, zombie organizations are pretty good at certain
decisions—the ones they are used to and have seen over and
over again. Their rules, their automation, their bureaucrats, and
their organization charts are designed for regular, repetitive decision-making. Therefore, zombie organizations can make some
significant progress—in one direction and without regard to possible opportunities or threats along the way (just like zombies in
the movies who go by silent, dark houses where the humans are

hiding [opportunity!] or walk right up to people with shotguns [threat!]).

Organizations today face many more decisions, of greater variety, as they attempt to respond to, and ideally take advantage of, the VUCA-digital world and digital transformation; efficient and effective decision-making across a wide range of issues becomes really important. Smart organizations are good at doing that— and they think about how they make decisions, and how to make their decision-making better.

As we know, a decision is really a combination of a prediction (what you think will happen) and a bet (what time, effort, political capital, and money will be needed) you are prepared to put on that prediction. In zombie organizations, any novel or significant bet is funneled upwards. To a certain extent, this reflects the fact that organizational decision-making is another "flow system," to use Professor Bejan's terminology. He calls hierarchy "the design of life," and points to its ubiquitous use in human organizations for moving information and getting decisions made:

> Almost every government has one leader—the chieftain, king, sultan, president, prime minister, governor, or mayor—who, like the main river channel, must handle the most important flow of information and authority. He or she is assisted by a few streams of top advisers, who themselves work with and oversee the many individuals who form the bureaucracy. This same hierarchy, which is often described as "vertical integration" in the business world, defines the structure of most corporations (one CEO, a few top managers, many workers), universities (one rector or president, a few provosts and vice presidents, more deans, even more department heads, and

many more professors, teaching assistants, and students) and sports teams (one head coach, a few assistant coaches, many players).[146]

Hierarchy itself is often pointed to as "the problem": it is associated with limiting an organization's flexibility, slowing decision-making, and being where Dilbert's "Pointy-haired Boss"[147] rules and the Peter Principle ("In time, every post tends to be occupied by an employee who is incompetent to carry out its duties"[148]) is the law of the land.

I would argue that this is a misunderstanding of hierarchy. What we see in zombie organizations is not the result of hierarchy itself; instead, as we have discussed previously, it is the effects of Weber's "monocratic bureaucracy," Frederick Taylor's "scientific management," the closed organizational mindset, and the "closed-push-no-context" communication platform used in those organizations.

Zombie organizations have trouble making non-standard, novel, or "big" decisions. These tend to get "kicked up the ladder" and then get made either autocratically by The Boss—in a "the buck stops here" kind of way, or, more frequently, using a group-think-based, consensus-by-attrition, process. Either one likely results in slow and poor decisions. The Boss model results in poorer decisions because he (and it is most likely to be a "he"—and a tall, white "he" at that), has only limited information—since messengers coming to The Boss with "bad" news are regularly shot, there is—not surprisingly—a shortage of messages about "bad" news (known in smart organizations as useful "feedback").

Another reason for poor decision-making is that The Boss only has access to a limited number of perspectives on any one

U.S. CEOs of Fortune 500 companies are four times more likely to be six feet or taller than you would expect; and almost eight times more likely to be 6-foot-2 or taller.[149] And only 25 out of the same 500 companies are run by a woman (often in the retail and food production industries).[150] And only five are black.[151]

The only reason I can see for this is that our social, emotional brains lead us—boards of directors, executive recruiters, etc.—to act out deeply embedded stereotypes about what makes for a good leader.

problem—and a severely restricted amount of time to devote to any one decision. These two causes are interrelated; since all the significant decisions float up to him, he has a lot of thinking and understanding to do. But, because he has so many decisions, he must rely on trusted lieutenants to advise him (who themselves are overburdened). In order to be "trusted," these lieutenants tend to be like him—that is, white, male, tall, and with a similar background (same colleges, same sports affinities, etc.).

Or he relies on his own "gut"—which is basically internalized past experiences—itself built on limited feedback from the few messengers willing to take the risk of delivering anything but good news to him. Since he is a CEO, his gut must be right (and better than anyone else—especially those who are not a CEO). And perhaps it should be "He"—since many CEOs suffer from some form of a God complex (and, of course, we know psychopaths are four times more likely to be found in the ranks of CEOs than in the general population—albeit at only 4 percent versus the 1 percent you would expect). It seems likely to me that CEOs become CEOs much like one particular lightning strike starts a forest fire. That one bolt of lightning thinks, "I'm the One"—whereas in reality, there were lots of strikes before and after that just as easily could have set off the tinder-dry forest. There was nothing special about that one lightning strike—it just happened to be the one. So, for CEOs-to-be, it just so happened that one of the 6-foot-plus, white males who went to the right school and played the right sports, was in the right place at the right time (based on all his privileges)—and ended up as CEO. Nothing special about that one man—he just happened to be the one.

> God complex: "a person that has an un-moving mindset that he is infallible and not capable of being wrong or failing at any task no matter how difficult or daunting it might be."[152]

"The Boss" decision-making approach tends to be, on average, slow, because the flow of decisions is too much for one person (and his trusted coterie of sycophants) to handle. Like a dam in the river (or a clog in the drain), decisions get backed up while waiting for The Boss. Then, the decisions either become urgent enough to get pushed to the front of the line (with the decision then made too quickly), or the opportunity passes and the decision becomes moot.

Unfortunately, everyone across the organization, to the degree that they are exposed to his (gut) thinking, emulates his decision logic. Decisions that don't make it all the way up the chain of command are made by mini-The Bosses, who prefer not to make any decisions that won't, post facto, make sense to the CEO's gut.

The ancient proverb noted earlier, laid claim to by many cultures, seems to be true: "The fish rots from the head down" as The Boss' thinking either directly or indirectly leads the zombie organization in a one-minded direction.

Alternatively, in zombie organizations, decisions are made using a groupthink, consensus-by-attrition process. Leaders involved in a decision keep meeting and studying that decision until either groupthink takes over, or those involved are so tired of the process that they agree on the things they can all agree on (i.e., the lowest common denominator).

Groupthink, as we have seen earlier, is already likely to occur. But it is even more likely given that the leaders tend to be chosen for the degree to which they either directly or indirectly look like, and think like, The Boss. Consequently, women and ethnic minorities rapidly learn to go to the right schools and, in large organizations, to dress and pattern their behavior after the dominant male style.

You then find that everyone around the table likes playing golf or watching football or something like that. And all approach the prediction/bet in front of them from a similar perspective. Our social brain drives us to "fit in" with the group (and avoid any "nasty" alternative thoughts)—and groupthink dominates.

Then, the decision is to be implemented. But, these non-standard decisions typically require a cross-group implementation (e.g., Product Development working with Marketing and Operations; or the Policy people with the Field staff). This means that multiple leaders share some part of the responsibility for executing on the decision (or parts thereof)—but often no one actually feels overall responsibility. So, the new initiative bumbles along—often joining the ranks of zombie projects that are too important to kill, but not important enough to make successful.

And, of course, across both methods we see Slater's "clots of power or the sclerosis of hierarchy" emerging. Humans = social; and for humans, social = politics. In my view, politics, like hierarchy, are naturally occurring and useful in human society—if applied correctly. Politics are really about who gets to decide what; and the people who get to make the decisions tend to make the decisions that favor them (their status, their certainty, their autonomy). So, if just oligarchs decide things—as, for example, in Russia—you get decisions that favor them; if only partners in a big law firm get to make them (because clients don't push back and the market favors the law firms), then you get partner-centered decisions. Democratic societies—where the choice as to who gets to decide is fairly widely distributed—then (over time) you get decisions that are centered around the needs of a wider set of voters.

In zombie organizations, you get The Boss-centric decisions (there is a whole sub-branch of economics devoted to this so-called "principal-agent" problem) or, to the extent that the market allows it, internal-bureaucrat-centric decisions (which you often see in public sector organizations, where the performance of the organization is only tenuously linked to citizens' needs). These "clots of power" make the flow of decisions slow and poor.

Smart organizations, unlike zombie ones, understand that decision-making speed, quality, and efficiency are important; and that hierarchies have value if the right decision makers are correctly aligned. The questions, therefore, become not how to do away with hierarchies, but how to make the best use of them; and how to make decisions quickly, well, and with the least effort.

They do this in three main ways. First, they understand that, in addition to the organization chart hierarchy, there needs to be another mechanism to deal with the critical, non-standard decisions. Second, they work on making the decision-making process as transparent as possible for the widest set of participants possible. Finally, they have a wrapper of decision-process supports—such as templates, data services, facilitators, and decision models—to help make those decisions better, faster, and cheaper.

Zombie organizations, based on monocratic bureaucracy, use the military-style organization with a central-command model for decision-making with a fundamental emphasis on control. The organization chart outlines who reports to whom (i.e., who gives you your marching orders). Information is supposed to flow up (we have seen the limitations there), with decisions flowing down (typically a case of too little, too late—too little thinking, based on too little information, and too late to seize the day). It is no surprise then, that military metaphors abound in zombie organizations (we are in a "war for talent," marketplaces are "battlegrounds," competitors are to be "attacked").

Professor John Collier discusses how such military-style organizations maintain themselves—and how difficult that is to do:

> Both experience and the theory proposed here suggests that this sort of organization will require a lot of excess effort to maintain...To some extent, they must rely on predispositions in their populations, but largely they rule by terrorist methods and fear. This requires a large concentration of both...economic and political power, since driving a system artificially requires a lot of power and waste of energy...such states will be unstable. Unfortunately, whenever there are large concentrations of political, economic, or physical power, there will be a tendency to use forced entrainment of ideology, howev-

er inefficient. A more efficient, but less reliable method, is propaganda and advertising, which attempt to drive or create resonances through subtle forcing...Such a social system is always fighting a gradient towards more efficient organizations. This is one of the primary social lessons we can derive from complexity theory: forced control is unstable and expensive (wasteful).[153]

Zombie organizations use their political and economic power to force this entrainment (i.e., pattern of behavior). Everyone working in a zombie organizations understands that underpinning everything in the organization is an iron fist hidden under a velvet glove ("the organization will fire you if you don't obey or perform or meet the standards we set"). You see this as well in the classic motivational posters bought by organizations of soaring eagles (Leadership!) and people rowing boats (Teamwork!). These are part of a propaganda supporting an ideology designed to (not-so) subtly force entrainment with two key notions:

- Leaders are far-sighted—and have talons and sharp beaks

- Your job is to just pull on the oar—and not think too much![154]

Smart organizations understand that there are difficulties when trying to manage the polarities that are inherent in any complex organization: local versus national (or global); customi-

---

"Only the guy who isn't rowing has time to rock the boat."

—Jean-Paul Sartre[155]

zation versus standardization; and innovation versus exploitation. There is no "right" answer to these types of questions—just degrees of "rightishness" (or "wrongishness"). These polarities often arise when decisions have impacts across functional groups (e.g., Product Development and Marketing) and, even with the best

A RECIPE FOR A DECISION-MAKING BOTTLENECK

"At one automaker we studied, marketers and product developers were confused about who was responsible for making decisions about new models.

When we asked, "Who has the right to decide which features will be standard?"

64% of product developers said, "We do."

83% of marketers said, "We do."

When we asked, "Who has the right to decide which colors will be offered?"

77% of product developers said, "We do."

61% of marketers said, "We do."

Not surprisingly, the new models were delayed."

—Researchers Rogers and Blenko

will in the world, there is tension and conflict as different groups operate—as they should—with different goals and incentives.[156]

They understand that a hierarchy for decision-making improves the flow of decisions—but they also know that such structures can impede dealing with emerging issues. They understand that having decisions made at the lowest possible level means that the people closest to the issue or opportunity—who have the richest information on the situation—can make better predictions and bets. And, conversely, they understand that some supposedly "little" or "local" decisions can have major impacts (both positive and negative).

So, as we have seen in the previous chapter, smart organizations work to support "spontaneous entrainment" as a form of a "rising tide lifts all boats" kind of approach: They work to communicate and reinforce memes like open mindsets and the purpose to which the organization is dedicated.[157] This is partly why small start-ups can adapt so quickly—the founders clearly convey the purpose of the organization, learning is encouraged (minimally viable product is the watchword these days for start-ups), and the social-brained workers in those companies spontaneously align their behaviors and actions.

Smart organizations also understand that, beyond their regular organization chart (to be used to identify the person who gets to make a normal or standard decision), they also need a decision chart for high-value/risk and high-complexity decisions, which cross organizational silos with a matching decision process to go along with it. These decision charts and processes can be used at both enterprise level and business unit level.

Here's what the process would look like:

Process steps	Roles/notes	Example
Define the Decision Area	The Area describes the desired organizational outcome and nature of the problem/issue/risk as understood now; might be one-time or ongoing	Our organization needs to be more innovative than it is now
Assign a single person who will own the Decision area	The Decider is the person who makes and executes on the decision; he/she has responsibility for the prediction/bet's success or failure	Director of Innovation
Assign people—Participators—to help make the decision	Participators have organizational responsibility for some key part of the (possible) solutions or own all or part of the problem/issue	Director of IT (technology likely part of the solution(s); Operations Leader (owns outcome; also key resource—client service teams)

Director of HR (owns key resource—levers to change people's behavior)

CEO (key resource—owns leadership team) |
| Decider presents options and makes a recommendation to the Participators | Each Participator has one veto (with reasons); this encourages the Decider to accommodate their needs/interests | Action plan for starting series of innovation challenge with software including: changing some elements of the company's performance mgmt. system and leadership messaging/communications |

Process steps	Roles/notes	Example
Veto triggers CEO to appoint a Reviewer	Reviewer is someone not previously involved in the decision; Decider has one preemptive challenge on who that Reviewer might be	IT Director vetoes because of her concern about security issues
Decider and Reviewer work together to come to a joint recommendation	Decider is encouraged to satisfy the Reviewer—who is fresh to the issue—about the nature of the veto (but does not have to satisfy the objecting Participator him/herself)	Decider convinces Reviewer that, with slight modifications to the original proposed Decision, the security issues are sufficiently mitigated given cost of further mitigation and the business value
If no agreement, Decider and Reviewer present options to Business Unit leader/ CEO for his/ her final decision		Decision proceeds as modified with Director of Innovation responsible to ensure implementation; starts to think about next set of proposed Decisions

Of course, the open-mindset and fast-communication platform make this process so much easier. But smart organizations also work to make decision-making transparent. Such transparency both allows staff to contribute (as they have inclination)—adding more information and diversity to the decision-making process—and it ensures that the ultimate decisions made are more likely to be successfully implemented (since the staff are both forewarned and had an opportunity to contribute their perspective).

Smart organizations manage and publish the Decision chart (alongside the org chart) to the organization. The CEO and board of directors (or organizational equivalent) regularly review both charts to make sure that they continue to have the right people making the right decisions—both standard and "critical."

Finally, to make sure all the decisions are made as efficiently and effectively as possible (both critical and noncritical but "standard" ones), smart organizations use mechanisms to support that decision-making. They treat each decision, the "situation to be handled" in Karl Wiig's terminology, like a slippery, twisting "case" to be solved by you and your colleagues working as collaborative Sherlock Holmeses. As you work the case, you will gather background information and seek expert advice. You will need to look at the case from different perspectives and apply different mental models: Was it really a murder? Or an artfully contrived suicide instead? A gangland hit, or lover's revenge?

Like any good detective, you'll want to have a team workspace for you to discuss things with the team and keep the files of where you can find the information you gather. However, unlike a physical file, you will want this workspace to be digital. That means others can be added to the team as needed—and they can quickly come up to speed on the case. You will want the team to be able to have online conversations, held in the file, about what you are discovering, and to be able to share links to and leave comments on the documents and other materials you are collecting. Other digital decision workspaces, from other decisions, would be available to you and your team as a potentially rich source of information.

Your workspace will need to be digital for another reason: As you work the case, you will find the need to adapt your approach, and, as a consequence, restructure the information in it.

ADAPTIVE CASE MANAGEMENT

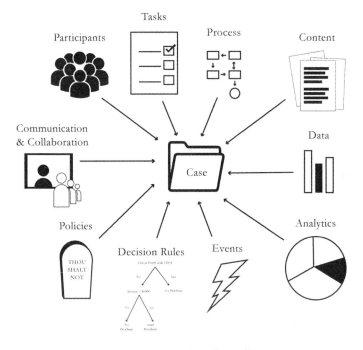

Figure 21: Digital workspace for cases[158]

This "adaptive case management" approach means you and your team will look for "pivot" points as your thinking on the case develops. With a flexible structure for your data (using links and tags) you can reorder, resort, and search through the material you've gathered, so you can look at the information from a new perspective.

Finally, unlike Sherlock Holmes, you will not want to work in secret, but will want your digital workspace out in the open. That way, others in the organization can find out what you are working on and, if they have something to contribute (a blog post they wrote, a spreadsheet with data they know about), they can easily share it with you.

A related decision support would be for the organization to develop templates for similar "cases." Such templates could include:

- Lists of suggested Participators for that kind of decision

- Materials providing decision frameworks (e.g., a draft point-factor evaluation set of criteria for a technology acquisition)

- Suggested meeting agendas with draft material (e.g., first team meeting)

Furthermore, a smart organization could develop a core set of common resources to support decisions, such as:

- Expertise location capabilities (e.g., search engine pointed at a set of information about the organization's staff)

- Data library with descriptions of the organization's data sources, their metadata structure, and contact/owner information (or enterprise data warehouse)

- Data analytic or modeling tools

- Training modules on decision-making (how to recognize different decision types; options for different approaches to decision-making; common pitfalls in decision-making; polarity management)

- Decision support team—providing guidance to the resources, training on decision-making and the functionality of the relevant software, facilitation as a service; consulting advice

The "adaptive case management"[159] approach is not difficult to implement. The digital workspaces are relatively cheap and easy to put together with existing technology (e.g., Yammer/Office 365; Atlassian Confluence with Jira; Jive with SharePoint). Organizations already have data sets—and data about the data sets. They already have trainers and internal consultants. It really is more a question of applying them to making the smart organizations' decisions better.

CHAPTER 8

Living in a post-zombie world:
What a smart organization looks like on the inside

The future is already here—it's just not very evenly distributed.

—William Gibson[160]

So, what would it be like to work in a smart organization? Are decisions really made more quickly? Is it more fun to work there—with playground slides and ping pong? Is there less deadwood taking up the oxygen? Are the bosses nice? Does stuff get done?

Perhaps Google is an example of a smart organization: It is consistently rated as not just one of the best technology companies to work for, but one of the best U.S. companies period, having placed in the top 10 "Best Places to Work" every year since 2012. Google's CEO, Sundar Pichai, is in Glassdoor's 2016 Top-10 CEOs list, with 96 percent of employees "approving" him.[161] And, of course, Google is immensely successful with the second-best brand in the world, according to Interbrand's 2016 ranking report,[162] and is one of the top five most valuable public companies in the world (sometimes number one, depending on the stock markets that week).[163]

Here's what some of the people who work at Google say about the experience—culled from just the first page of comments on the Glassdoor site:

"An environment that is conducive to growth and curiosity. Encouragement and support from all directions."

"A great culture that works best as a cohesive unit, rather than individuals."

"Best environment for fostering creativity. Allowed for good team bonding and stent strategic partnerships amongst colleagues...Cons:...Management focused on results at times vs. process or accuracy."[164]

And this is what Google says about who they are looking for when they hire:

...people who can bring new perspectives and life experiences to our teams. If you're looking for a place that values your curiosity, passion, and desire to learn, if you're seeking colleagues who are big thinkers eager to take on fresh challenges as a team, then you're a future Googler.[165]

Apple, also a top company for financial success and a company that people hope to work for, has a description with a similar flavor of who they like to hire:

We're perfectionists. Idealists. Inventors. Forever tinker-
ing with products and processes, always on the lookout
for better...a job at Apple will be demanding. But it also
rewards bright, original thinking and hard work. And
none of us here would have it any other way.[166]

All of us know what it is like to work in a zombie organization. Now let us imagine what it would be like to work in a smart
organization—what would an "average" day be like for someone,
let's call her Suzi, who is in middle management in an organization called SmartOrg, Inc. today? Here's her story:

*Suzi had to go into the office today. Mostly she worked from
home, or in a local coworking location (where she went
when she needed to get away or wanted other people around
her). But there was a big, in-person meeting with her Participators as a kick-off to her first Decision as a Decider.*

*There were the kids to get up and get moving (where
did that knapsack get to?); but, in between dressing herself and monitoring their progress, she used her smartphone
and checked the Decision's digital workspace to see if there
were any last-minute updates or questions that she needed to
deal with. All the Participators had checked into the digital
workroom—and most of them had at least opened the slide
deck (she could tell from the "visitors" list). One of them,
whom she knew well, had left her a private message: "All
the best today!"*

*There was another comment, left by Hamed, a Par-
ticipator she didn't know well, at slide 6; he had asked
about whether the numbers there were year-to-date or for*

the previous financial year. The good news, Suzi thought, was that he had read the slides carefully; the bad news was that she was 99 percent sure they were for the preceding 12 months—but she needed to check to make sure. She quickly responded to the comment:

> *@Hamed—thanks for the comment. I'm going to ask @David to check and #RUSH get back to you.*

By doing so, Hamed would know they were working on it, and her numbers guy, David, would get a notification (in the digital workspace application, or by text or email depending on his preferences). And the rest of the team wouldn't be interrupted, but would see, when they next looked at the workspace app (on their phone or on their laptop), the message on their #RUSH list about what was happening and who was doing what.

Her partner had made the coffee (thank you!), which was usually her job (somehow she made better coffee). While she sipped from her mug (everyone in the household knew to wait until she was at least halfway through the caffeine before trying to talk to her), she thought she would check, one more time, the task board for her Decision. The board had almost a hundred cards on it with various tasks that they had identified: Many, she noted with satisfaction, were in the "Done" column, but most were scattered across the other "states of the work" columns:

- *Ideas—a parking lot for suggestions for work they might need to do*

- *Owner?—for work they had decided to do, but no one had responsibility for yet*

- *Doing*

- *Holding—where they were waiting for someone outside of their team to get back to them*

- *Finalizing—used when a document or other item had some finishing details or required a signature*

- *Done*

There were a lot of cards in both the "Ideas" and "Owner?" columns—the team had an online brainstorming session the previous week to look at the work ahead following the kick-off meeting. It looked like a couple more cards had been added to the "Ideas" column since then; it was easy to spot them since the "unread" cards were highlighted. She glanced at the new ones briefly and saw that a couple came from people she didn't know. The board was available organization-wide, and the new cards had come from people who had suggestions for the team. Once they were through today's meeting, Suzi thought, they would go through all the tasks in "Ideas" and "Owner?" at their next daily team stand-up meeting, then figure out which ones to do and who was going to do them.

But, for right now, Suzi need to drink more coffee (sip... Ah!). She then clicked on the "meeting-date" tag to filter the board so it just showed the tasks related to today's big meeting. All the cards were in "Done," with just the "room set-up" card—with its checklist—in the "Finalizing" column. That particular task was templated and cross-posted to the facilities team's board for their building. They used it to do their part of the setup. A change in the checklist on the card (e.g., adding clip-on microphones) automatically showed on both boards and was highlighted as "unread" for each team member. Of course, the task owners (there were two—one on her team and one on the facilities'—were notified directly).

With one card for two teams, there were no slip-ups as things changed (as they constantly seemed to), and everyone always had the most recent version in front of them.

She flew out of the house and headed to work. As she sped along—as much as the traffic allowed—she reviewed how the Decision, her Decision, got started. It had long bugged her that, while the organization was open to new ideas for products and services, there didn't seem to be any "regular" way to do that; and that she had seen some pretty good ideas get lost in the shuffle. Partly because the company had been growing quickly, and with new people and new acquisitions over the last 18 months, everything was a bit shambolic; and partly because the organization wasn't as good as it ought to be in collecting and understanding customer feedback.

She thought, and had started complaining about it often enough, that there should be some sort of pathway for people to follow when they had an idea for developing something, and that there should be some supports for people to do that. Then one day, two months ago, the CEO had published a blog post about some of the most recent new products/services. She had replied to the post with a comment about this gap and some of her thinking about how to close it. Her VP had seen it—she was one of Suzi's followers, or maybe she had seen it through the #innovation hashtag—and sent her a private message encouraging Suzi to propose a Decision.

⸻

Suzi was looking for a new challenge; she had just rolled off a big project and, when she looked at her "My Stuff" board (a summary of all the task cards she owned across all the boards in the organization) she could see she had some room for this (especially since the new person on her team was turning out so well and looked like he could take on higher-level work). She knew, if the organization decided to move ahead, that this would be challenging both for her personally and for the organization. For her, it would mean having to manage some tough conversations with some senior players—something she didn't have a lot of experience with. But she knew that the organization valued people who stretched themselves (even if things didn't quite work out); and she had taken to heart something she had heard during her on-boarding. It was a quote from the French novelist Jean Giraudoux: "Only the mediocre are always at their best."

To start the Decision she had gone to the organization's intranet, or internal website. Basically, the organization consisted of four things: processes, decisions, resources, and people. If it was a standard, repeatable thing, with a work-flow you could find the processes (like changing your address) and get it done. Anyone could create a process, but most were created and maintained by various teams.

Most of the work in the organization was a "Decision"; again, anyone could click the button in the intranet and create a decision workspace. Suzi had done that when she

"Only the mediocre are always at their best."[167]

started to explore the idea of creating an organization-wide product/service development capability. After she clicked the button, the system had asked her for a title, brief description, and to choose what kind of decision she was working on. She had chosen the "explore idea" template, and the workspace was set up.

It had a couple of handy things already in it, including:

- *A listing of links (with brief descriptions) of the last 10 decision workspaces that had used that same template (in case someone else was already working on that kind of idea)*

- *Search results:*

  - *from the company's resources (i.e., documents, data sets, the website) using terms that it had extracted from her title and description ("product development," "service development," "innovation," and "customer feedback")*

  - *from the company's "people" information— basically anyone who had those terms in their biography, or had used those terms in any blog post or comment or work item that they owned*

- *A task board with some suggested tasks that included things like "identify people you know who could contribute," "identify people who you DON'T know who could contribute," and "find a decision coach"—as well as cards focused on organizing the first Decision meeting*

- *A list of "how to make a decision" resources that included online tutorials, decision hacks like the KJ Method, and a list of decision coaches (people the organization had identified with experience in guiding the organization to make a broad range of decisions, and were on-call to help anyone with their decision)*

Suzi thought she could use some help, so she had looked at the list of coaches. She checked out the bios on a couple of people; she found one that she sort of knew and thought would be a good fit. But, when she looked at that coach's current workload (she could see his "my stuff" board), it looked like he was slammed. Then she spotted another coach with a lot of experience in this kind of ambiguous, multi-stakeholder, type of decision-making. She used the link on "find a decision coach" to fill out the simple request form and send it to her.

Over the next couple of weeks, a number of people had "joined" her workplace and taken on (or been assigned) tasks as she worked towards getting this Go/No-Go decision about whether the organization wanted to take on this Decision. They had created a definition of the problem, drafted a prediction of what would happen to the organization without doing anything, and proposed the initial "bet"—to spend the internal time (plus a little bit of money for some consulting advice) to investigate options. And that proposal was what was going to the Decision meeting today.

The meeting was the first item on her calendar for the day. She had just half an hour as she got to the office before it started to see if @David had answered the question. She saw that he had found the right data set, checked with the data owner (she had been right; it was the rolling 12 months), had updated both the slides to make them clear (everyone had a link, so if they went back to it they would see the corrected version), and he had mentioned @Hamed to let him know the answer. Now she was ready.

She was excited, and just a bit nervous, going into the meeting. She expected, as at all of the organization's meetings, that the attendees would want two things: to make a good decision for the organization (since everyone "got" the purpose and wanted the company to be successful); and for her to be successful (even if that meant taking some company time and money to try out something that may not work).

The discussion was hotter than she had expected—a couple of her Participants thought the organization was currently overburdened and this just added to it—and others thought that the current, flexible, "none" structure was working well enough. But by the end of the 90 minutes, she had the go-ahead to work on the Decision. That meant that she would take the Decision all the way from developing options, to getting the Decision made, and through implementing the decision itself (including, if necessary, adding or reallocating budgets and people, and purchasing services or products). She had a lot of work ahead of her.

She did three things as she got back to her office after the meeting: First, she sent an @All message to everyone in the decision workspace with the news and included the hashtag #epic. Messages with that hashtag were available across the company—that way, everyone would see her thank you to the team and could celebrate the achievement of this milestone. Most people seemed to enjoy hearing about successes and subscribed to that hashtag. Often, people reading the messages would add their own comments of encouragement.

Second, she sent David a message in the workspace saying:

"@David—thanks for jumping on that question; by double-checking with the data owner you reduced our risk of getting it wrong and avoided wasted time in the meeting (or worse, getting the decision wrong) #feedback"

Next time she had a chance to meet with David, she would, as she did whenever she met with her staff, review all the #feedback messages they had sent or received. That way, she was constantly giving—and getting—feedback.

The third thing was to check her email to see if anyone from outside the organization had sent her anything. All of her internal messages came through digital workspaces, and she basically lived there during the day. It was so much easier to pull what she needed, in the workspaces with all the info she needed at hand, than it used to be when they used emails and attached files. Today, there was one email from a consultant that might be helpful to the Decision.

The afternoon was a whirlwind of meetings—mostly online—and starting some processes and some additional decision workspaces. One of those was the selection of a consultant to assist in the baseline assessment that the work plan called for. It wasn't a big decision, but it would be helpful to have one place to store all the information she collected about the firms, the people, and the types of consultants out there. There was a "hire a consultant" template for the workspace, so that made it really easy. She grabbed the email she had received that day from the consultant and put it in the folder "Possible consultants." The consultant had named one of her colleagues as a reference, so she @messaged that person asking about him.

She was tired but happy as she headed home. She couldn't have imagined getting as far as she had in her old company, which used email to organize and share what was going on, where people seemed to be looking for mistakes (rather than successes), and where getting a decision made was a constant struggle.

Suzi's day, and a day like it for everyone in the organization, 365 days a year, is more than possible. It is doable, today, for every organization—and with less effort and cost than zombie organizations are putting in to maintaining their current, outmoded, and fundamentally repressive systems.

What is different inside a smart organization that makes days like Suzi's possible for everyone working there? You can start anywhere in the alphabet soup of acronyms we use for the different functional groups that help the organization operate, such as HR, IT, S&M, KM, OD, L&D, GRC, PMO, and AP.

These groups commonly provide some combination of three things:

- Compliance—figuring out what rules apply to the organization and helping it adhere to them (e.g., when HR ensures compliance with local human rights codes during hiring)

- Service delivery—making things happen that the organization needs to have done (e.g., when HR assists in finding candidates for job vacancies and organizes the interview process)

- Strategy—understanding how the world is changing related to their functional perspective, and what the firm can do to mitigate the negative effects or seize the opportunities resulting from those changes (e.g., when HR sees that recruiting for talent is becoming more competitive, and it starts working to build the organization's brand among high-value potential employees using social media)

They will still need to do all these things—but some of their programs and the way they operate will need to change. Here are some examples of how a couple of key functions—HR, IT, KM, and S&M—need to change:

Human Resources
Performance management

As we have seen in an earlier chapter, zombie organizations' performance management systems are based on several key assumptions that are false. We now know that:

- There are many more "high performers" than the bell curve allows for

- People are emotional and social, not rational and individualistic

- SMART goals degrade performance

"The best use of money as a motivator is to pay people enough to take the issue of money off the table: Pay people enough so that they're not thinking about money and they're thinking about the work."

—Author Daniel Pink[168]

Smart organizations have rethought their reward-and-recognition systems to take this set of understandings into account. Some of the things they do include:

- Ensuring fair pay for everyone as a starting point

- Focusing attention on helping employees identify and build on their individual strengths, while aligning their work to the goals of the organization

- Training everyone how to give and get feedback on their performance

- Increasing the volume, frequency, diversity, and richness of that feedback (e.g., as Suzi's organization does by using the #feedback hashtag)

- Measuring the effectiveness of the performance management system

Human Resources
Leadership selection and development

Who is at the "head"—and how they act (and whether they "rot")—is paramount in any organization. Leadership selection and development is critical.

Every time an organization chooses a new leader—from frontline manager to CEO—it is placing a significant bet. There is the time and effort to select and train the new leader, and there is lost productivity as they come up to speed; but the biggest part of the bet is the impact the new leader can have on the degree of staff engagement, and his or her contribution to shaping the organization's ecosystem (more on that in the final chapter, where we discuss smart organization leadership).

One big change for HR in smart organization is the work to collect and analyze data on the quality of those selection bets. To avoid the Peter Principle (every job is ultimately filled by a person incompetent at the work), different kinds of data need to be collected to improve the organization's assessment of possible leadership candidates' suitability for leadership (or for the next level of leadership).

Leadership development also needs to become more data-driven (so that developmental opportunities can be evaluated for their cost-benefit ratio). A "mass customization" approach needs to be used in the design and delivery of development opportunities; that is, since there is no "average" leader, development programs must become much more tailored to the individual's strengths and weaknesses. Finally, there should be opportunities to connect with and foster relationships across the leadership team built into the development activities. This engenders trust between the leaders, improves their understanding of how the rest of the organization works, and accelerates knowledge-sharing across the group.

Everyone in the organization, but especially leaders (or want-to-be leaders), should keep a personal decision workspace where they can keep all the information about themselves, including feedback they receive, notes on coaching or mentoring they have received, and a task board for the personal improvement work they want to do as they make predictions and bets on how they should develop. Leaders can use this information to make decisions about their own life and career—and parts of it can be shared and used as a kind of portfolio during a leadership selection process.

Finance
Budgeting

Budgeting is a system for making prediction and bets. It makes the prediction about what is going to happen next year—and places bets on where the organization should spend its money. Zombie organizations look backwards at historical operational spending and, based on that information, project forward with a focus largely on cost-savings. Separately, there is some sort of investment or project budget where quantified projects with known ROI or some sort of "keep-the-lights-on" component (e.g., IT infrastructure upgrades or regulatory compliance) are preferred. Managing the budget is a key part of any leader's SMART goals (going over budget is definitely not going to get you the key "1" rating).

Unfortunately, such an approach creates a straitjacket for the organization. Any existing business unit has more or less "locked in" funding that creates a disincentive for change (either growth or reduction), while freezing out any possible new business units (since all available funding is soaked up by the existing units). Likewise, with the project budget, once the keep-the-lights-on and "clear" ROI projects are counted up, there is typically little money left over for any additional projects with significant possible benefits but are hard to quantify or have higher risk.

Smart organizations still have budgets, but shift the focus from retrospective and cost-containment to prospective and value-enhancement. The focus for leaders is on adding value—not necessarily hitting a budget number that was locked in up to 12 months (or maybe more) before. Operating units would undergo a staggered, zero-based review every three to five years (depending on the size and complexity of the organization). There are two different "investment" budget pots—one for "must-do" (but not value-adding) projects, and the other for value-adding projects. The latter money would be held in a pot that could be accessed during the year for emerging opportunities, and provide seed money to prototype a speculative idea (and build the business case for it) and scale-up money to take a successful idea enterprise-wide.

Finance
Expenses

Processing expense claims is one of those standard corporate irritants that seem to beget more and more rules—with more and more rule-checkers. The result is frustration for those trying to get expense claims paid, and cost to the organization for this burdensome overhead.

To provide guidance to those with expense claims, smart organizations use a wiki that is cowritten by those who have expenses and those who are responsible to make sure the spending is aligned to the organization's purpose. All expense claims should be processed without checking—unless there are certain "flags" that come up (e.g., amounts over a threshold or for certain items that might be inappropriate). Where claim-submitters are consistently raising flags—i.e., seemingly not understanding or following the guidance—their expenses would shift to a "preapproval" required basis. That way, compliance efforts can be focused where they are needed.

Finance
Transparency

Budgets in zombie organizations tend to be "hidden," with few people knowing where all the money is going. Smart organizations make the organization's spending patterns available to everyone in the organization (obviously in a way that ensures personal privacy, and without divulging extraordinarily confidential information such as a legal settlement payment).

Along with budget information, of course, smart organizations internally publish any operating metrics they have. With this level of transparency, employees can contribute in a meaningful way to the ongoing decision-making (predictions and bets) regarding "would a dollar spent here be better than a dollar spent there?"

Information Technology
Managing access—inside/nearside

One of the challenges for IT departments is that much of the decision-making work of organizations will require more fluid "borders" between those who are "inside" the organization, and those who are not employees, but are trusted nearsiders in some way.

These could be alumni (employees who had previously worked in the organization, but have now gone on to somewhere else), or trusted suppliers, or well-known contractors, or stakeholders of the organization.

These nearsiders are extremely valuable to smart organizations; since they know the organization well, and share (or shared) its purpose, they can significantly extend the breadth and number of people who contribute to sense-making by "scouting" on behalf of the organization. Furthermore, they can be direct contributors to decision-making. For example, experts from a software vendor could be included in a decision workspace related to how to make better use of the software.

And, of course, there are valuable software and datasets that employees within the organization will want to bring "inside" (or at least have access to or interact with). This poses a challenge to IT departments who are rightly worried about identity and access management, cybersecurity, and maintaining confidentiality. IT departments in smart organizations need to work to make it possible for more porous boundaries between people and datasets.

Information Technology
Pilots and trials

IT in smart organizations is also much better at pilots and trials, since more of these will take place as staff in all parts of the organization explore different technologies (to improve the way they operate, or to understand the impact of emerging technologies on business models).

Knowledge Management
Metadata

Many organizations have some kind of knowledge-management function that traditionally has focused on collecting and organizing content (like best practices or templates) so that it is easier and faster for staff to retrieve them. Many organizations have also invested in search engines that can be pointed at this metadata along with other content (e.g., corporate systems like CRM), and so return search results that make it easier to find individual pieces of content as well as to create composite views of a topic (e.g., a customer) that is assembled from multiple sources.

Underlying this function is the creation and maintenance of consistent information about the content (e.g., the office location for Hong Kong is always "Hong Kong" and not other variants like "HK" or "China-HK"). Users can filter data based on specific criteria (in this example, office location) to find what they need.

By adding digital workspaces and shifting conversations out of emails, the amount of content to be organized and searchable has grown significantly. This will be a challenge for existing KM teams.

Knowledge Management
Decision-management (DM)

More profoundly, instead of thinking of themselves as managing knowledge, these teams should see themselves as managing decision-making. That is, they need to be DMers, since the key that organizations need is not so much organizing knowledge (which is important), but accelerating the gathering and creation of knowledge in service of making predictions and bets. KM teams seem to be best-placed to support that activity in such activities as managing the underlying metadata structure, spotting the need for new decision-making templates, optimizing the search engine, and ensuring profiles for participants are useful and up-to-date.

Marketing/Sales
Customer/client feedback

One extraordinarily important source of feedback to the organization is from customers or clients of the organization. Zombie organizations tend to prefer not to interact with customers or clients; perhaps once every six to 12 months, someone will conduct interviews with them or send out a survey or hold a focus group. A report about the results is prepared and sent up the line; confirmation bias from groupthink—such a powerful force—would make sure the report is simply restating some version of what the organization already knows. And, even if the report does contain new information, zombie organizations are adept at ignoring or discounting any bad news.

Smart organizations, in contrast, love to get feedback from customers and clients about the products and services, about the experience of interacting with the organization, and about ideas from them regarding new products and services. These organizations go out of their way to first create a sense of identification with the organization, and then engage customers in contributing to shaping the future of the organization. Starbucks, for example, has a website—http://mystarbucksidea.force.com/—set up for customers to "Share. Vote. Discuss. See." product, experience, and involvement ideas.

Marketing and sales teams are going to need to get their heads around how the organization might do this for their customers or clients. This goes well beyond just having the website with the requisite functionality that supports the required activities (posting, commenting, voting, etc.); it also requires a committed set of participants who understand and support the organization, and it requires the organization to handle and respond to invariable criticism of decisions the organization makes.

Marketing/Sales
Alumni networks

Previous employees, "alumni," frequently go on to become purchasers, competitors, suppliers, or regulators of the organization. They are an invaluable source of information about what is going on in the industry and the wider world because they understand the organization (how it is structured, how it thinks), but now have a different perspective.

In zombie organizations, at best, past employees merely drift away with no sense that they are "alumni"; at worst, they are given the sense that they somehow betrayed the organization by leaving and are now shunned by it. Smart organizations encourage former employees to remain feeling connected to it; they invite the "alumni" to return for events, send them updates on what the organization is doing, and encourage them to participate in sharing ideas or information with the organization. Along with current customers and clients, these alumni are an important source of information and feedback that take considerable care.

CHAPTER 9

Hot rebooting a zombie organization:
The soft stuff is hard

The difficult tasks of the world
Must be handled through the simple tasks
The large tasks of the world
Must be handled through the small tasks
Therefore, sages never attempt great deeds all through life
Thus they can achieve greatness

—From the *Tao Te Ching*, Chapter 63[169]

Starting an organization with a new "smart" operating system shouldn't be that hard. That's how Google and Apple, our earlier examples of smart organizations, did it. But how do you fundamentally transform an existing zombie organization's operating system—its mindset, its communication platform, and the way it makes decisions? How do you manage that while the organization is still running and operating? And how do you keep the new operating system alive while the old, zombie one reacts to it like your immune system does when it detects intruders in your bloodstream?

The great political thinker Machiavelli, writing nearly 500 years ago in *The Prince*, understood the problem well. He said this about how hard it is to make change—and why that is:

> ...it ought to be remembered that there is nothing more difficult to take in hand, more perilous to conduct, or more uncertain in its success, than to take the lead in the introduction of a new order of things. Because the innovator has for enemies all those who have done well under the old conditions, and lukewarm defenders in those who may do well under the new. This coolness arises partly from fear of the opponents, who have the laws on their side, and partly from the incredulity of men, who do not readily believe in new things until they have had a long experience of them. Thus it happens that whenever those who are hostile have the opportunity to attack they do it like partisans, whilst the others defend lukewarmly.[170]

A more modern thinker, Salim Ismail, who is Dean of Singularity University and who wrote the book *The Exponential Organization*, says this about innovating within an organization:

> In a big company, when you try to do disruptive innovation, the immune system of the company will come and attack you. All the work structures are built to withstand change and withstand risk.[171]

So, are the enemies of the "new order"—those who have "done well" under the zombie operating system—destined to win? I don't think so. I believe those of us who want to build smarter organizations can win—but it is, as Machiavelli pointed out, difficult and by no means certain. It can also be perilous.

Why perilous? Because that immune system response, if triggered within the organization, will be aimed directly at you. One study, of employees who were seconded full-time into a change agent role as part of a reengineering program at a large hospital, found that over half of the respondents were promoted after their role ceased.[172] That sounds pretty good.

However, I do wonder about the other half—what happened to them? And, remember, these employees were in a role paid for by the organization and engaged in sanctioned change. They were not generating change so much as overseeing the communication of change that had already been determined. When looking at advice on how to get promoted, I have yet to see one that says the way to get ahead is to "challenge the existing orthodoxy and leadership." The contrary is much more likely, typified by David Goldin, founder and CEO of Capify, who had this advice for how someone in their 20s could get promoted: "Trust the process, and show you can focus on playing by the rules instead of fighting them."[173]

That immune system response will be a powerful one that operates at every level. For example, one innovation leader arrived at his to-be team's new workspace to find, instead of an empty space where they could create a dynamic work environment, a delivery truck about to unload a set of standard-issue cubicles. Calls had to be made up the chain of command to get the delivery stopped (since SMART goals required the on-time delivery of new furniture to any new workplace). Then, two weeks later, the same cubicles arrived to be delivered all over again. Why? The furniture team's manager had changed—and the new one wanted to make sure he was making his numbers. Another round of calls had to be made to get that stopped—again![174]

It is useful to understand where this resistance comes from. To have read this far in this book would suggest a reader is interested, even passionate, about transforming organizations. It is likely you would not be like those resisting this change. Abraham Lincoln gave some good advice on this: "I don't like that man. I must get to know him better."[175] Behind that resistance is a certain logic; and, if we hope to create change in organizations, we must first understand it.

Partly it comes, as Machiavelli has pointed out, because certain people do well under the current system. Remembering the SCARF model; they enjoy their status, they have autonomy within the system (in some cases, those highest up the hierarchy are very autonomous), they are "related" to those similar to themselves, and they would think it unfair to lose their privileges. The other reason is that they have great certainty—the "C" in the SCARF model—that what they are doing, and what the organization is doing, is the "right" way. Most everything they see around them, from the business press they read to the conferences they attend, and even embedded in the software they use (like email), reinforces that this way is the right way. So, their brains build neural networks around this default operating mode (neuroscientists describe this as "what fires together wires together"), reinforced by the social group (of similar people) around them. As a result, they have a hard time grasping that perhaps another reality is in play. At worst, perhaps some leaders are suffering from the cognitive bias called the Dunning-Kruger Effect, whereby individuals are unable to recognize their own ineptitude[176] (what Rumsfeld would call an "unknown unknown"—i.e., the individual doesn't know that they don't know).

The other thing is that these resistors of change are partly right—maybe only 10 percent—but there is more than a grain of truth in what they say about the dangers, the cost, and the pain involved. That is because organizations are caught between two polarities: between structured and unstructured, being "closed" versus "open," or, to put it another way, change and stability. They cycle around some equilibrium point that lies between being more open to change or with more of a focus on stability and standardization.

Each pole of the polarity has an upside and a downside; there is no actual "right" answer as to whether it is better to change or to be stable—it depends on the demands of the environment that surround it at that time. All organizations need to be able to do both—to have change AND stability.

Here's how that polarity looks[177]:

CHANGE-STABILITY POLARITY

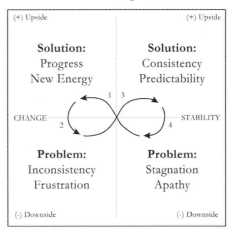

Figure 22: Change management from polarity perspective[178]

If organizations can manage this polarity successfully, they can continue to compete and meet the needs of customers or clients. Zombie organizations are stuck at an equilibrium point nearer to the Downside of stability—stagnation and apathy; they need to shift their equilibrium towards Change with its upside of progress and new energy.

The good news is that all organizations have within them, perhaps deeply buried, some experience with change and some desire for progress and energy. Someone wanting to reboot a zombie organization can make use of that inherent part of the zombie's thinking as a way to avoid triggering the immune response. The story of the introduction of sushi to North America could be instructive. Now ubiquitous, sushi first faced an enormous uphill battle to become accepted in the United States and Canada. It had three strikes against it: it was raw, it was fish, it was foreign. But some chef (there is debate as to who it was) thought up the California Roll, which combined familiar ingredients in a new way and provided a gateway for sushi to become the gigantic part of the food industry it is today.

Nir Eyal, author of *Hooked: How to Build Habit-forming Products*, coined what he calls the California-Roll Rule: "People don't want something truly new, they want the familiar done differently."[179] So, for transforming an organization, you need to present the "new" change as something familiar, but just done differently. For example, when bringing in the new communication open-pull platform, you can say it's like email—it's just done differently.

You can also use the thinking behind polarity management to acknowledge that the fears of the resistors have some foundation. Simply doing so can take a great deal of energy out of their resistance. You could say something like: "Yes, you are right, there will be some disruption. What would you suggest we do to mitigate that risk while moving forward with the change?"

Many change management programs put an emphasis on communicating about the change, which does make sense. But it is important that such communication be structured to take into account the SCARF reactions of those involved. For example, if you constantly communicate that things are really, really going to be disrupted, then it is hardly surprising that you trigger a "withdraw"—and hostile—response to all the uncertainty. And, if you don't move quickly enough, you provide resistors with enough time to organize themselves and to (in Machiavelli's words) "attack like partisans."

It is important to realize that it is difficult to marshal sufficient resources—time, energy, internal political buy-in, dollars—to be able to directly push an organization to make profound change. Direct pushing on people tends to lead to something—but rarely the action you were hoping for. It is equally important to understand that organizations are nonlinear systems with a multiplicity of interacting subsystems with multidirectional interactions between them. In such systems, as Jeffrey Goldstein in his book *The Unshackled Organization* put it, "change can be precipitous and revolutionary." [180]

Moving from a zombie operating system to a smart one is certainly "precipitous and revolutionary." If direct pushing (even if you have the resources) won't do it—then what will? You want to use the natural, social-copying tendency that people have (remember our social brain) so they want to join in on the "new." Changing the organization's narrative (i.e., the stories that people tell and hear) about what is going on, what is possible, and what people want, can have a profound impact on people's willingness to embrace the "new."

We humans like our consistency—and our brains are unhappy when we are doing things that are inconsistent with what we believe. This state—of cognitive dissonance—is really uncomfortable for us. So, we try to avoid it as much as possible by either changing our beliefs or our actions. Here's how Emily Lawson and Colin Price, partners at the consulting firm McKinsey, explain the implications for organizations:

> ...if its people believe in [the organization's] overall purpose, they will be happy to change their individual behavior to serve that purpose—indeed, they will suffer from cognitive dissonance if they don't. But to feel comfortable about change and to carry it out with enthusiasm, people must understand the role of their actions in the unfolding drama of the company's fortunes and believe that it is worthwhile for them to play a part.[181]

There are a number of elements to this: First, there is the need to engage employees so they understand and are aligned with the purpose of the organization, because our social nature drives us to be connected to others; second, employees must be helped to see how they play their part; third, they must trust that the organization has, at least to some degree, the best interests of the employees at heart; and, finally, they must believe that change is possible (i.e., that any effort they put in will not be in vain).

If your organization is, for example, part of the military, or delivers medical supplies in emergency situations, it's pretty easy for employees to understand the "purpose" of the organization. But what if you work for a soft drink company? Or you are an accountant at one of the Big Four? What is their purpose (aside from making shareholders or the partners richer)? Every organization exists to meet a human need of some sort—organizations just need to think through and articulate them. Coca-Cola Bottling Co. has—their stated purpose is "To Honor God in All We Do"[182] but they also articulate another, secular purpose that almost everyone could support: They say that their company "provides moments of happiness for millions of people every day."[183] For accountants, one of the Big Four firms, Deloitte, says that "Our desire to make a positive, enduring impact every day for our organization and its stakeholders requires that…We contribute to society, *building confidence and trust, upholding integrity,* and supporting the community."[184] [emphasis added] If accountants and soft drink peddlers are doing it, then you can as well.

By connecting the change entailed in your zombie makeover to that larger organizational purpose, you help reduce that cognitive dissonance. You make this connection by telling stories and sharing pictures. No, this is not kindergarten; but humans have a 40,000 year history of using images to communicate,[186] and at

Figure 23: Lascaux cave art (17,300 years old)[185]

least as long a history of telling stories. We know from neuroscience research that stories activate the whole brain. Why would that be? Because, as the great pattern-seekers that we humans are, we look for cause and effect. More importantly, it is the only way that one human can activate a listener's brain so that the idea or experience becomes their idea or experience.[187]

And, of course, you can tell your story (of becoming a smart organization) to many people at the same time. A good story teller, speaking the language of the listener, can couple her mind to theirs: Her ideas, her desires, and her experiences become theirs. Uri Hasson, associate professor of psychology at the Princeton Neuroscience Institute, explains what his research has discovered:

> The more listeners understand what a speaker is saying, the more closely their brain responses mirror the speaker's brain responses...I'm generating a brain wave that generates a sound wave that generates a brain wave in you. There's nothing mystical about this. It's not a Jedi mind trick. This is what communication is. It is what humans do best, and it's unique and amazing.[188]

Then, you want to work to spread these "new" stories—really about the familiar done differently—through peer-to-peer networks. Basically, you are working to create a viral entrainment, using stories, around the desired "smart" behaviors that already existed but were overlaid by the "zombie" behaviors.

"It's not a Jedi mind trick. This is what communication is. It is what humans do best..."

—Uri Hasson

Vice President Al Gore did precisely this with his "Climate Reality" project, which recruited (through social media) and trained Climate Reality Leaders to better tell the story of climate change and inspire communities everywhere to action.[189] The people taking the training were so inspired by Gore's PowerPoint slide story that they paid for the opportunity to tell the story themselves. Political campaigns—such as the recent Clinton vs. Trump U.S. presidential election—are examples of candidates and campaign teams trying to tell a compelling "story," get certain ideas into people's brains, and encourage a peer-to-peer network to take that story to more and more people.

Not all "peers" are created equal. So, you particularly want to focus on trying to entrain the (real) high performers that you have. You will want to foster this distributed leadership (remember, you have many more high performers than you thought you had).[190] They are easy to find: Just ask around in any part of the organization for the person to turn to when something tricky needs to get done, *and* that person is "nice." They may or may not be in a leadership position; they may or may not be experienced; but they are most likely (prediction!) a high performer that you could work with (bet!) to effectively share the organization's "smart" story.

To be clear, the story is not about "I am right and you are wrong," because that will throw the reptilian part of brain, the amygdala, into fight-or-flight mode. This is what happens in zombie organizations when people are told, or voluntold, to do or believe something. As David Rock, leadership consultant, and Jeffrey Schwartz, research scientist at UCLA, put it: "The traditional command-and-control style of management doesn't lead to permanent changes in behavior. Ordering people to change and then telling them how to do it fires the prefrontal cortex's hair trigger connection to the amygdala. The more you try to convince people that you're right and they're wrong, the more they push back."[191] A similar thing happens when organizations use the "burning platform" approach: It makes people feel uncomfortable and it raises their anxiety, creating stress and resistance. Many of the "best practices," innocently used by those trying to drive change in organizations, use a top-down or fear-based approach that treats people as objects to be pushed around. Such approaches are counterproductive.[192]

These are the secrets you can use as you embark on remodelling your organization from a zombie operating system to a smart one: Employees want to be connected—to others, directly and through the purpose of the organization, and to the rest of the organization indirectly. Your idea of a smart organization can be implanted in them through your stories and images. They, in turn, can share the story with others.

Look around your organization—both the physical and the symbolic—to see what images are there, hiding in plain sight, that reinforce (or undermine) the telling of your smart story. As we have already discussed, posters of soaring eagles and rowing teams detract from the "smart" story, as do cubicle work spaces. It is unlikely that you'll be able to replace the office furniture—but look for opportunities in the flow of change within organizations to influence what happens next with your story. For example, if your HR department is starting a review of their leadership development program, try to introduce your story to them and look to collaborate with them to shift that story forward in some way.

The great thinker Marshall McLuhan famously said: "We shape our tools, and then our tools shape us."[193] So, as organizations start shifting over their communication and decision-making "tools" to something familiar yet different, these tools will start shaping zombie organizations into smart ones. Email, as a tool, has shaped zombie organizations to be closed (secretive) and "push"-based—with people telling other people what to do and how to think. Open-pull communication systems are inherently transparent and collaborative; they will "shape" the behavior of people within smart organizations by encouraging transparency and allowing employees to pull the stories they want to hear.

Likewise, within zombie organizations, our reliance on the tools of hierarchy, silos, and decision-making ad hocery, has shaped people within those organizations. In those organizations, you defer to those above you, toe the line as you stay within your silo (and expect others to do the same), and play "follow the leader" in making any decision. With the familiar, but different, smart organizations tool to make Decisions (focused accountability, planned broader involvement, managed objections), zombie organizations will be changed into smart ones.

Tom Peters, the well-known business author (best known for his book *In Search of Excellence*), once said: "I think the soundest management advice I've heard is the old saw; 'What gets measured gets done.'"[194] I think it is good advice. What would you need to measure to get the zombie change done? Your change efforts are a set of predictions and bets; you need to know whether they have been successful (or not)—so that you can adjust the model you are using to understand the organization and, therefore, adjust your tactics.

One simple measure is to keep track of the number of times you hear the "smart" story you created now told by someone else in the organization. Some form of the "smart" story is, to some extent, already circulating—so you'll want to establish a baseline and look for growth in that number. Keep track of the number of different people who tell the story, and in how many offices or functional groups they come from. This gives you an idea of the diffusion of the story.

At the beginning, with your new open-pull communication system, simply look for usage: how many people, how many logins, how many page views, how many comments or uploads or other activity, how many groups formed or topics started. That will not come without a struggle, as people will naturally want to stay where their relationships are, and where the content is—i.e., in email. Email is essentially built into all of a zombie organization's work practices, so you will need to help the groups involved to reimagine those practices to take advantage of the new communication capabilities.

For example, something as simple as a team update meeting can be transformed by using the new platform. These meetings are a way to share information on who is doing what, and what issues (or opportunities) have arisen. But, with the open system, the work is already on the board, and the conversations about issues or opportunities are available to be pulled at any time. So, the team meeting needs to be reimagined in such a way that it is more about what to do next and how to do better (rather than exchanging information); and, as a result, can be shorter and a lot more interesting. You can measure meeting time (number of people multiplied by length of meeting) and email volume—both will go down in smart organizations.

Improvements in the design of the organizational decision-making flow are hard to measure directly. It would be nice to measure the velocity, size, and quality of the decisions flowing through the organization's decision structure, but that can be a lot of effort given the tremendous variability in nature of the decisions. Ultimately, of course, these faster and better decisions will result in all sorts of positive outcomes, like improved share price, higher satisfaction scores, reduced insurance premiums, etc.—but those are all very much lagging indicators. Perhaps the best proxy, then, is to conduct a survey and look for employees' perception as to how fast and good they think the organization's decisions are today—and then repeat that survey every six to 12 months to see the improvement.

You can do the same thing regarding a desired shift in mindset. You figure out the behaviors that you are looking for in a smart organization, and then survey people about to what extent they see those behaviors around them. Be careful not to ask them about their own behavior—that is too threatening and you won't get any useful information. But do regularly ask employees what they observe in the behavior of their peers and leaders, and look for change over time.

You are looking, as the *Tao Te Ching* advises, to "Achieve large tasks through the smallest tasks." Look for where the smart, desired organizational behavior already shows itself. Be aware of what is happening, and look to accelerate serendipity by taking advantage of an unintended consequence of some action or a crisis.[195] Then see how you can nurture and protect it.

TAO TE CHING: "ACT WITHOUT ACTION"

Figure 24: PLAN, PICTURE (圖 = Tu)[196]

The soft stuff is the hard stuff—not because it is hard to do, but because it has hard, profound effects. Organizations are yearning to be smart, as are the people within them. Your job, as a zombie killer, is simply to help the inner smart organization come out.

CHAPTER 10
Leadership judo in a zombie organization: How to lead your organization back to life

The philosophers have only interpreted the world in various ways. The point is to change it.

—Revolutionary thinker Karl Marx
(incised in gold letters on his gravestone)[197]

Being a leader, in our VUCA-digital world, is no longer some version of a reality show entitled "How to Become the Top Dog—and Stay There." The world is too different today. As General S. McChrystal, commander of the International Security Assistance Force and U.S. Forces in Afghanistan, put it in his book *Team of Teams*: "We have moved from data-poor but fairly predictable settings to data-rich, uncertain ones;" and he goes on to say: "I began to view effective leadership in the new environment as more akin to gardening than chess."[198]

> "We have moved from data-poor but fairly predictable settings to data-rich, uncertain ones."
>
> —General S. McChrystal

Uncertain times call for smart organizations that can process that data and make prediction/bets; and, in so doing, become resilient. But zombie organizations are brittle—they are unbending for a time, and then suddenly break (or get swallowed up). That rigidity comes from being stuck nearer the Stability pole, and being reluctant to engage with new information and new ideas. Professor Jeffrey Goldstein, in his book *The Unshackled Organization*, says:

> The nonlinear, circular structure of self-fulfilling prophecies keeps an organizational system at equilibrium. This nonlinear cycle creates a barrier around work groups and organizations that keeps them isolated and closed-off to new information or new ways of interacting with their environments. The self-fulfilling prophecy has the power to do this because it is self-confirming—its own beliefs reinforce themselves by way of actions congruent with those beliefs.[199]

In a zombie organization, no one says, like the child about the naked Emperor in Hans Christian Andersen's children's story, "but he isn't wearing anything at all"; and the illusion of stability is maintained in an unsustainable equilibrium.

How can that be? The people in those work groups, and across zombie organizations, remain isolated because they do not have "psychological safety." A two-year study by Google, looking at over 180 teams, found that this was by far the most important of the five team-effectiveness dynamics they discovered. As Julia Rozovsky, one of the study researchers and a Google people operations analyst, said about it: "We're all reluctant to engage in behaviors that could negatively influence how others perceive our competence, awareness, and positivity."[200]

You will recall that, in Andersen's story, no one says anything about the Emperor's lack of clothing because they were afraid of being seen as "unfit for their positions, stupid, or incompetent."[201] In the same way, within zombie organizations, we each stay locked inside our own little work groups. People stay within the group's "norm"—i.e., do not consider new information, new ideas, and new connections—because they are attracted to their (from the SCARF model) Status, Certainty, and Relatedness to others. So, by our words and actions in the group, we reinforce the current thinking; and we can see that the engine of Goldstein's self-fulfilling prophecy is psychological safety fueled by Status, Certainty, and Relatedness.

How, then, to lead people out of this? Instead of brute (political) force and a "father-knows-best" approach, leaders hoping to transform their zombie organizations need to think differently—indeed, "be" different. Judo—a combat sport—offers part of the answer. The word "judo" comes from two Japanese characters, and literally means the gentle ('ju') way ('do').[202] It involves using balance, movement, and leverage. Author and physical trainer Philip Shapira describes how it works: "Skill, technique, and timing, rather than the use of brute strength, are the essential ingredients for success."[203]

So, a leader looks within her zombie organization for momentum and leverage points that she can use. The work of the leader from this perspective is to amplify the existing tendency towards change inherent in the organization's Stability-Change polarity. But where do you find the judo leverage points? And, given that organizations are nonlinear, complex, adaptive systems, how can you know the outcome of whatever it is that you might try?

Dave Snowden, developer of the Cynefin Framework, neatly summarizes the approach leaders take to both change into, and maintain, a smart organization: "We manage the emergence of beneficial coherence within attractors, within boundaries."[204] The goal of a smart-organization leader, therefore, is to work towards this "beneficial coherence," which, for a smart organization, is a new equilibrium point within that Stability-Change polarity. That point consists of an ever-morphing set of individual and organizational behaviors which enable better (faster and higher-quality) organizational decision- (prediction- and bet-) making.

There are, as Snowden explains, three ways to manage this emergence:

Constraint management, removing or creating constraints to allow new possibilities to emerge...

Coupling...How tight is the coupling [with whom and with what]? Can we allow for novel connections to form virtually or physically which will change the properties of the system?

Catalysts introduced can institute new patterns of behavior, attractors can emerge as a result...or boundaries dissolved or shifted from being rigid to permeable.[205]

The role of a smart-organization leader is to shape an organization's internal ecosystem using its own energy and interests. She nudges rather than orders; she coaches rather than corrects; she is constantly observing the situation and seeking feedback on her "catalysts," "constraint management," and her changes to "coupling." To be successful she must combine theory and practice to come up with prototypes of "probes" regarding the design of the organization's information and decision flow systems. Since the system is complex, she is never sure what might happen; she must constantly observe and reflect on what she sees. This approach combines strategic opportunism with efforts to accelerate positive serendipity.

General McChrystal took (what I have called the smart organization approach) to organizing his forces: He "restructured our force from the ground up on principles of extremely transparent information-sharing [what we call 'shared consciousness'] and decentralized decision-making authority ['empowered execution']." He saw, as we heard earlier, that this new approach to the organization required a new model for leadership (or should we call it gardenership?):

The move-by-move control that seemed natural to military operations proved less effective than nurturing the organization—its structure, processes, and culture—to enable the subordinate components to function with 'smart autonomy.'[206]

Our leader-gardeners could employ tactics that aim to inspire, to nurture, and to model; and, of course (as the new beneficial behaviors become apparent), to work to embed them. When modeling, they should encourage prototypes and small-scale experimentation to help identify what works (involving key stakeholders, if possible). When they see what works, they should nurture it by looking for ways to amplify, scale, and extend it (to other areas of the organization, either geographic or functional). As they do so, it is important to keep checking back to see the impact on the "smart" mindset and decision-making flow.[207]

One powerful catalyst, as we have discussed earlier, is the use of stories. Jurgen Habermas, the great sociologist and philosopher, describes this as a "communicative action":

> Whereas in strategic action one actor seeks to influence the behavior of another by means of the threat of sanctions or the prospect of gratification in order to cause the interaction to continue as the first actor desires, in communicative action one actor seeks rationally to motivate another by relying on the illocutionary binding/bonding effect (Bindungseffekt) of the offer contained in his speech act.[208]

But, given their experience with zombie-organization leaders' fundamentally manipulative carrot-and-stick approach heavy with doublespeak (e.g., "rightsizing," "realignment," "pursuing other opportunities," "challenge," "job flexibility"[209]), staff are naturally suspicious of anyone attempting to "lead" them to new information or new ways of interacting. For this communicative action—storytelling—to entrain the listener, the listener must feel safe and must trust the storyteller. And so, the smart organization leader must be completely transparent in what she does; how else would anyone trust her and her motives—and with it, her "story" and their interpretation of any changes she was leading? Without that trust, no entrainment is possible (the triggered amygdala will make sure of that).

So far we have been talking of a leader; the reality, however, is that this leadership is much more a group act than a solo one. The first order of business of any smart organization want-to-be leader is to find others who have the same sense about the Emperor that she does: There is something rotten in the state of Denmark, and an alternative future is possible for the organization. This group of leaders must work together to manage this emergence. Andrew Millstein, president of Walt Disney Animation Studios, describing the creative team that worked on the movie *Frozen*, provides a good description of how they should work:

> Creativity needs time, space, and support to fully explore multiple ideas simultaneously. Our creative leadership has to have the confidence and trust in each other to experiment, fail, and try again and again until the answers to story questions and problems get better and more refined.[210]

A smart leader lives a work-life of praxis as she acts, studies, and reflects on both. In doing so, she herself changes. She is part of the organization's system—it acts on her as she acts on it (in unanticipated ways). A smart organization leader is constantly morphing. She tries to understand her own strengths, her thought patterns, and her weak spots in both. To do so, she constantly seeks out feedback from those around her (and is able to provide it, constructively, to others). She takes that feedback, and her reflection on it, to build her awareness of when she overuses a strength (and experiences its shadow-side) and underutilizes strengths she can develop and better apply. She continues to refine the mental models she uses—understanding that they are only a more-or-less accurate facsimile of the changing world around her.

Smart organization leaders share many characteristics. One that requires special notice is their ability to be vulnerable. It takes someone very brave to say that the Emperor has no clothes, or, at least, "I don't know the answer to that," or "I made a mistake." It takes real courage to be vulnerable because it triggers what Brené

Brown calls our "master emotion"—the fear that we are not good enough. Men in particular "walk this tightrope where any sign of weakness elicits shame, and so they're afraid to make themselves vulnerable for fear of looking weak."[211] But it is this act of vulnerability that truly makes for a smart organization leader—and this vulnerability that builds trust and connections with others. We can see the truth in what Goldstein and his colleagues have written: "The locus of leadership is in interaction; thus, leadership is truly a verb not a noun."[212]

> Bridgewater Associates—which manages $150 billion of global investments in two hedge funds—uses "getting to the other side" when reviewing an investment gone wrong: "What is it about how you—the responsible party and shaper of this process—were thinking that might have led to an inadequate decision?"
>
> Their CEO models vulnerability—and sent a company-wide email with the subject line: "I fail every day."[213]

Smart organization leaders know that, no matter what their personal characteristics, the undertaking they are involved in will take considerable time and effort. It is more a marathon than a sprint. Self-care will be very important—both body and mind. It is trite but true to say that they must make sure to eat well, exercise, and get lots of sleep. Just as important, smart organization leaders know they need strong social connectedness—with family, friends, and co-workers—to help them not just survive, but to flourish in what will be one of the most exciting and fulfilling times of their working lives to date.

Besides vulnerability and self-care, some of the other characteristics you will observe in a smart organization leader include:

- Highly tolerant toward ambiguity

- Has personal integrity

- Self-aware and reflective; listens to her intuition

- Practices mindfulness

- Observant and skilled in deep listening

- Passionate about getting and giving useful feedback

- Feminist—supportive of diversity and inclusion (and able to check her own privilege)

- Culturally fluent (so as to be accepted across organizational silos)

The list appears overwhelmingly long and seems to require someone of saint-like qualities. At a basic starting point, gardener-leaders must at least understand the business and understand people. Unfortunately, the news here is not good: In a study of 60,000 managers, less than 1 percent of them were considered to be in the top third of performers for both those attributes (if you look at the top half, you still find only 5 percent).[214] On the upside, there is not much competition for what, I believe, will be high-demand characteristics.

Why not get started? Perhaps you are not feeling quite ready; perhaps there is an alternative path—like staying in your "track" by keeping your head down and playing by the rules. That path is clearly laid out for you—so why not take it (even if the ultimate result is less attractive to you) since the other way seems to be unclear and full of potholes? Author Robert Brault has an interesting perspective to offer on this question: "We are kept from our goal not by obstacles but by a clear path to a lesser goal."[215] Do not confuse a simple way forward with it being the better way forward.

You will never feel fully ready. I wasn't ready to write this book—but I did. The best advice I received on this topic I pass on to you. It comes from writer (and Psychology Ph.D. candidate) Benjamin Hardy, who wrote these words of wisdom:

- "Give yourself a timeline to act"

- "Act sooner than you're ready...Listen to your intuition"

- "Get yourself into a peak or passionate state, and make committed decisions from that state"

- "The highest rewards are not material, but purpose-centered"

- "Make the decision. Commit to the decision"

- "The longer you wait, the longer it will take to get where you want to go. The opportunity cost of procrastinating...is enormous"[216]

Organizations run the world. They can be so much better—instead of being zombies, they can be smart. And, when they become smarter, the people working inside them have richer, better, and more fulfilling lives. Think how much better the world would run with smart organizations. Imagine helping engage all those people in their work. Don't you want to be part of that? Lead your zombie organization back to life—as a smart organization.

CODA

Steps to lead your zombie organization back to life

Here are some suggested steps you can use to lead your zombie organization back to life.

Note: The order is only a rough guide, and is not intended as a recipe (that would be impossible, given the nonlinear nature of organizations).

1. Go to www.BuildingSmarterOrganizations.com to join our merry band of zombie fighters and access additional resources

2. Calculate your organization's "Z" score

3. Share your "Z" score with others in the organization and ask them to complete it; discuss the results with them and reflect on your own scoring

4. Connect outside of your organization to other Building Smarter Organization (BSO) leaders

5. Assess your own personal strengths and goals (e.g., take the free Values-in-Action Strengths assessment: https://www.viacharacter.org/www/)

6. Engage an ICF-certified professional coach who is familiar with the strengths assessment you used

7. Start before you are ready

8. Share your goal(s) with others you trust—within and outside of the organization

9. Look to build a coalition of like-minded BSO leaders within your organization

10. Work on a "smart" organization story—with pictures—about what the change could mean

11. Identify leverage points—i.e., where and when the organization is opening up systems and processes or displaying symbols (e.g., town-hall meetings)

12. See if you can influence those who "control" those leverage points

13. Step back and see what impact you (and others) are having

14. Measure your success (e.g., number of "smart" story retellings you hear)

15. See if your organization is already using (to some extent) an open-pull communication software system, and learn how it works

16. Look to see how you can nurture and expand the organization's use of the open-pull communications software

17. Display some personal vulnerability at least once a day

18. Look at your daily work using an adage attributed to Dwight D. Eisenhower: "What is important is seldom urgent and what is urgent is seldom important."[217]

19. Schedule in time during your day for the "important" BSO work

20. Read, look, reflect—on what you are doing, could do, and the impact it is having

21. Conduct a survey asking people to report on the behavior they see (is it zombie-like? Or smart-minded?)

22. Let me know how you are doing by sending me an email at Gordon@BuildingSmarterOrganizations.com or by coming to the website

23. Continue forward

ENDNOTES

1. Henry Mintzberg. (n.d.) *Wikiquote*. Retrieved from https://en.wikiquote.org/wiki/Henry_Mintzberg.

2. Browne, A. (2016, August 15). The Specter of an Accidental China-U. S. War. *Wall Street Journal*, Retrieved from http://www.wsj.com/articles/the-specter-of-an-accidental-china-u-s-war-1471329372

3. Our leap into the unknown threatens both Europe and the world economy. (2016, June 26). *The Guardian*. Retrieved from https://www.theguardian.com/business/2016/jun/26/leap-unknown-threatens-europe-global-economy-brexit-greenspan

4. Ezrati, M. (2014, June 18). How America can overcome the challenges of an aging population. *PBS Newshour*. Retrieved from http://www.pbs.org/newshour/making-sense/how-america-can-overcome-the-challenges-of-an-aging-population/

5. Stoddard, Ed. (2016, August 8). Workers at S. African power utility Eskom strike over pay, supplies stable. *Reuters*. Retrieved from http://news.trust.org/item/20160808142344-gxrnw/

6. Sears tanked because the company failed to shift to digital. (2016, August 26). *BI Intelligence*. Retrieved from http://www.businessinsider.com/sears-tanked-because-the-company-failed-to-shift-to-digital-2016-8

7. Thompson, B. (2015, July 21). Aggregation Theory. Retrieved from https://stratechery.com/2015/aggregation-theory/

8. McDeavitt, J.T. (2014, December 23). Medical Education: Toy Airplane or Stone Flywheel? *Wing of Zock.* Retrieved from http://wingofzock.org/2014/12/23/medical-education-toy-airplane-or-stone-flywheel/

9. Internet Growth Statistics. (2016, November 24). Retrieved from http://www.internetworldstats.com/emarketing.htm

10. "Fourth Quarter 2015 State of the Internet Report," Akamai Technologies as reported in and retrieved from http://www.netimperative.com/2016/03/global-internet-speeds-23-just-one-year/

11. Google's mission is to organize the world's information and make it universally accessible and useful. *Google Company.* Retrieved July 26, 2016 from https://www.google.com/about/company/

12. As quoted in Nordhaus, W. D. (2016, August 18). Why Growth Will Fall. *New York Review of Books.* Retrieved from http://www.nybooks.com/articles/2016/08/18/why-economic-growth-will-fall/

13. Nordhaus, W. D. (2016, August 18). Why Growth Will Fall. *New York Review of Books.* Retrieved from http://www.nybooks.com/articles/2016/08/18/why-economic-growth-will-fall/

14. Miller, R. (2016, July 5). Letting Central Banks Manage the Economy Might Not Be So Bad. *Bloomberg.* Retrieved from http://www.bloomberg.com/news/articles/2016-07-05/brexit-like-populist-pressure-may-spawn-70s-style-stagflation

15. Larson, N. (2016, September 21). UN urges policy overhaul amid economic slowdown. *Yahoo News.* Retrieved from https://www.yahoo.com/news/un-urges-policy-overhaul-amid-economic-slowdown-192851047.html

16. How Digital Transformation Will Affect Business Over Next 3 Years. (2015, November 9). *MHL News.* Retrieved July 29, 2016 from www.mhlnews.com/

17.   Anthony, S.D., Viguerie, S. P., Waldeck, A. (2016, Spring). Corporate Longevity: Turbulence Ahead for Large Organizations. *Innosight*. Executive Briefing. Retrieved from https://www.innosight.com/wp-content/uploads/2016/08/Corporate-Longevity-2016-Final.pdf

18.   Anthony, S.D., Viguerie, S. P., Waldeck, A. (2016, Spring). Corporate Longevity: Turbulence Ahead for Large Organizations. *Innosight*. Executive Briefing. Retrieved from https://www.innosight.com/wp-content/uploads/2016/08/Corporate-Longevity-2016-Final.pdf

19.   Autor, D.H., Price, B. (2013, June 21). "The Changing Task Composition of the US Labor Market: An Update of Autor, Levy, and Murnane (2003)." *MIT Economics*. Retrieved from http://economics.mit.edu/files/9758

20.   Autor, D.H., Levy, F., Murnane, R.J. (2003, November). "The Skill Content of Recent Technological Change: An Empirical Exploration;" *Quarterly Journal of Economics*. 118(4); Revised from September 2002. Retrieved from https://www.mckinseyquarterly.com/Preparing for a new era of knowledge work 3034?srid=520

21.   Welch, J. (n.d.). *Wikiquote*. Retrieved November 24, 2016 from https://en.wikiquote.org/wiki/Jack Welch.

22.   Crabtree, S. (2013, October 8). Worldwide, 13% of Employees Are Engaged at Work. *Gallup*. Retrieved from http://www.gallup.com/poll/165269/worldwide-employees-engaged-work.aspx

23.   Fermin, J. (2014, May 26). Personality Traits of a Disengaged Employee. *Officevibe*. Retrieved from https://www.officevibe.com/blog/infographic-disengaged-employee

24.   Talk: George Carlin (n.d.) *Wikiquote*. Retrieved November 24, 2016 from https://en.wikiquote.org/wiki/Talk:George Carlin

25.   Hemp, P. (2004, October). "Presenteeism: At Work—But Out of It." *Harvard Business Review*. Retrieved from https://hbr.org/2004/10/presenteeism-at-work-but-out-of-it

26. "Managing presenteeism: a discussion paper." (2011, May). *Centre for Mental Health.* Retrieved from https://www.centreformentalhealth.org.uk/managing-presenteeism

27. Chui, M., Manyika, J., Bughin, J., Dobbs, R., Roxburgh, C., Sarrazin, H., Sands, G., Westergren, M. (2012, July). "The social economy: Unlocking value and productivity through social technologies." *McKinsey Global Institute.* Retrieved from http://www.mckinsey.com/insights/high_tech_telecoms_internet/the_social_economy

28. Silverman, R.E. (2012, December 11). Workplace Distractions: Here's Why You Won't Finish This Article. *Wall Street Journal.* Retrieved from http://www.wsj.com/news/articles/SB10001424127887324339204578173252223022388?mg=reno64-wsj&url=http%3A%2F%2Fonline.wsj.com%2Farticle%2FSB10001424127887324339204578173252223022388.html

29. Innovation. (n.d.) *Wikiquote.* Retrieved November 24, 2016 from https://en.wikiquote.org/wiki/Innovation

30. Drucker, P. (1994). "The Theory of the Business." *Harvard Business Review.* September-October 1994.Retrieved from https://hbr.org/1994/09/the-theory-of-the-business

31. Swenson, K. *Designing for an Innovative Learning Organization.* (n.d.) Retrieved from http://kswenson.workcast.org/2013/swenson_EDOC_2013.pdf

32. Fishburne, T. (n.d). "Helping GrowthCloud Communicate Ways To Grow With Their Clients." Image. Retrieved from https://marketoonist.com/campaigns/all/growthcloud

33. Verjovsky, A. & Phillips, J. (2016). *Outmaneuver: OutThink, Don't OutSpend* [Kindle version]. Retrieved from Amazon (n.d.) Retrieved from http://web.mit.edu/~dcltdw/AOW/6.html

34. Tzu, Sun. (n.d.) Retrieved from http://web.mit.edu/~dcltdw/AOW/6.html

35. Silver, N. (2015), *The Signal and the Noise*. New York, NY: Penguin Books; p. 17

36. Vigen, T. (n.d.). Spurious Correlations. *Tylervigen.com*. Retrieved from http://tylervigen.com/spurious-correlations

37. As quoted by Begneaud, S. (2016, March 14). Meet Your Brain, the Pattern Recognizing Machine. *Xdesgin*. Retrieved from http://www.thinkx.net/blog/meet-your-brain-the-pattern-recognizing-machine-friday-at-four

38. Milner, G. (2016, June 25). Death by GPS: are satnavs changing our brains. *The Guardian*. Retrieved from: https://www.theguardian.com/technology/2016/jun/25/gps-horror-stories-driving-satnav-greg-milner

39. Ku, G. "Auctions and Auction Fever: Explanations from Competitive Arousal and Framing." (2000). *Kellogg Journal of Organization Behavior*. Retrieved from http://citeseerx.ist.psu.edu/viewdoc/download?doi=10.1.1.196.9975&rep=rep1&type=pdf

40. Crumbaugh, L. (2015, March 23). Sunk cost fallacy: Throwing good money after bad. Retrieved from https://www.linkedin.com/pulse/sunk-cost-fallacy-throwing-good-money-after-bad-lee-crumbaugh

41. Staw, B., Barsade, S, Koput, K. (1997, February). "Escalation at the credit window: A longitudinal study of bank executives' recognition and write-off of problem loans." *Journal of Applied Psychology*, Vol 82(1), pp. 130-142. Retrieved from http://haas.berkeley.edu/faculty/papers/stawbarsade.pdf

42. Gerbert, P., Gauger, C., Steinhäuser, S. The Double Game of Digital Strategy. (2015, October 16). *bcg.perspectives*. Retrieved from https://www.bcgperspectives.com/content/articles/business-unit-strategy-big-data-advanced-analytics-double-game-digital-strategy/

43. Box, G. E. P. (1979). "Robustness in the strategy of scientific model building", in Launer, R. L.; Wilkinson, G. N., *Robustness in Statistics*, Academic Press, pp. 201–236. As quoted in: https://en.wikipedia.org/wiki/All_models_are_wrong

44. McClure, D. (2015, October 12). Why Lean Enterprise Transformation is Hard. *Medium*. Retrieved from https://medium.com/featured-insights/why-lean-enterprise-transformation-is-hard-ede266e1c973

45. Aghina, W., De Smet, A. Weerda, K. (2015, December). "Agility: It rhymes with stability." *McKinsey Quarterly*. Retrieved from http://www.mckinsey.com/insights/organization/agility_it_rhymes_with_stability

46. Johnson, B. (1998, September). "Polarity Management: A Summary Introduction." *Polarity Management Associates*. Retrieved from http://www.jpr.org.uk/documents/14-06-19.Barry_Johnson.Polarity_Management.pdf

47. Heffernan, M. (2015, May). Forget the pecking order at work. *TEDWomen 2015*. Video. Retrieved from http://www.ted.com/talks/margaret_heffernan_why_it_s_time_to_forget_the_pecking_order_at_work/transcript?language=en

48. Bolman, L.G., Deal, T.E. (2011). *Reframing Organizations: Artistry, Choice and Leadership*. San Francisco: Jossey-Bass. Retrieved from https://books.google.ca/books?id=nP_dYskywcYC&printsec=frontcover&source=gbs_ge_summary_r&cad=0#v=onepage&q&f=false

49. Taylor, F. (1911). *Scientific Management*. pp. 129-30. As quoted and retrieved from http://www.skymark.com/resources/leaders/taylor.asp

50. Cohen, P. (2012, November 19). America is still a patriarchy. *The Atlantic*. Retrieved from http://www.theatlantic.com/sexes/archive/2012/11/america-is-still-a-patriarchy/265428/

51. See various Dilbert comic strips for more.

52. Taylor, F. (1911). *Scientific Management*. pp. 129-30. As quoted and retrieved from http://www.skymark.com/resources/leaders/taylor.asp

53. Six Sigma. *Wikipedia*. Retrieved from https://en.wikipedia.org/wiki/Six_Sigma

𝄐

54. Bartlett, C.A., Ghoshal, S. (1990, July-August). "Matrix Management: Not a Structure, a Frame of Mind." *Harvard Business Review*. Retrieved from https://hbr.org/1990/07/matrix-management-not-a-structure-a-frame-of-mind

55. Bartlett, C.A., Ghoshal, S. (1990, July-August). "Matrix Management: Not a Structure, a Frame of Mind." *Harvard Business Review*. Retrieved from https://hbr.org/1990/07/matrix-management-not-a-structure-a-frame-of-mind

56. Attributed to "an outside consultant" in Coleman, J. (1995, November-December). A Quest to be the Best. *Measure*. Published by Hewlett Packard. Retrieved from http://www.hp.com/hpinfo/abouthp/histnfacts/publications/measure/pdf/1995_11-12.pdf

57. Ordóñez, L.D., Schweitzer, M.E., Galinsky, A.D., Bazerman, M.H. (2009). "Goals Gone Wild: The Systematic Side Effects of Over-Prescribing Goal Setting." Harvard Business School. Working Paper. 09-083. Retrieved from http://www.hbs.edu/faculty/Publication%20Files/09-083.pdf

58. McGregor, J. (2013, February 14). The corporate kabuki of performance reviews. *The Washington Post*. Retrieved from https://www.washingtonpost.com/national/on-leadership/the-corporate-kabuki-of-performance-reviews/2013/02/14/59b60e86-7624-11e2-aa12-e6cf1d31106b_story.html

59. Baer, D. (2013, February 21). Performance Anxiety: Why Reviews Hurt Everybody. *Fast Company*. Retrieved from https://www.fastcompany.com/3006089/performance-anxiety-why-reviews-hurt-everybody

60. Lagace., M. (2008, July 7). Innovation Corrupted: How Managers Can Avoid Another Enron. *Working Knowledge*. Harvard Business School. Retrieved from http://hbswk.hbs.edu/item/innovation-corrupted-how-managers-can-avoid-another-enron

61.   Brunker, M. (2014, June 25). Performance Mismanagement: How an Unrealistic Goal Fueled VA Scandal. *NBC News.* Retrieved from http://www.nbcnews.com/storyline/va-hospital-scandal/performance-mismanagement-how-unrealistic-goal-fueled-va-scandal-n139906

62.   Cunningham, L., McGregor, J. (2015, August 17). Why big business is falling out of love with the annual performance review. *The Washington Post.* Retrieved from https://www.washingtonpost.com/news/on-leadership/wp/2015/08/17/why-big-business-is-falling-out-of-love-with-annual-performance-reviews/

63.   Sohani, S.S., Varkkey, B. (2015, October). "Breaking Free From the Bell Curve: An Alternate Proposition for Performance Management." *Indian Institute of Management.* W.P. No. 2015-10-04. Ahmedabad, India. Retrieved from http://www.iimahd.ernet.in/assets/snippets/workingpaperpdf/6096466172015-10-04.pdf

64.   Duggan, K. (2014, June 17). Why Your Business Should Never Grade on a Curve for Performance Management BetterWorks blog. Retrieved from https://blog.betterworks.com/never-grade-on-a-curve/

65.   O'Boyle Jr;, E. Aguinis, H. (2012.) "The best and the rest: Revisiting the norm of normality of individual performance" HRMA Research Briefing. Based on an article by the same title in *Personal Psychology.* 2012, 65, pp. 79 - 119. Retrieved from http://www.hrma.ca/wp-content/uploads/2012/11/rb-the-best-and-the-rest.pdf

66.   As quoted in Hough, L. (2015, August 24). Beyond Average. *Harvard Ed Magazine.* Retrieved from https://www.gse.harvard.edu/news/ed/15/08/beyond-averag1e

67.   "Image from Design Learning from the Extremes." *Personalize Learning.* (2013, July 2). Retrieved from http://www.personalizelearning.com/2013/07/design-learning-from-extremes.html

68.   Engler. S. (2016, February 18). A Brief History of Why Performance Management Fails to Improve Performance. *CEB Blogs.* Retrieved from https://www.cebglobal.com/blogs/a-brief-history-of-why-performance-management-fails-to-improve-performance/?business_line=human-resources

69.   Kropp, B. (2015, September 9). Why Performance Management is Failing Your Best Employees. *CEB Blogs.* Retrieved from https://www.cebglobal.com/blogs/hr-why-performance-management-is-failing-your-best-employees/?business_line=human-resources

70.   Rock, D., Davis, J., Jones, B. (2014, August 8). Kill Your Performance Ratings: Neuroscience shows why numbers-based HR management is obsolete. *Strategy+Business.* Autumn 2014, Issue 76. Retrieved from http://www.strategy-business.com/article/00275?gko=c442b

71.   Ewenstein, B., Hancock, B., Komm, A. (2016, May). "Ahead of the curve: The future of performance management." *McKinsey Quarterly.* Retrieved from http://www.mckinsey.com/business-functions/organization/our-insights/ahead-of-the-curve-the-future-of-performance-management

72.   Bolte Taylor, J. (2008). *My Stroke of Insight: A Brain Scientist's Personal Journey.* New York: Viking.

73.   Rock, D. (2009, December). "Managing with the Brain in Mind." *Oxford Leadership Journal.* Vol 1., No. 1. Retrieved from http://isites.harvard.edu/fs/docs/icb.topic1331850.files/Social%20Dynamics/Managing%20with%20the%20Brain%20in%20Mind.pdf

74.   Rock, D. (2008). "SCARF: a brain-based model for collaborating with and influencing others." *NeuroLeadership Journal.* Issue one. Retrieved from http://web.archive.org/web/20100705024057/http://www.your-brain-at-work.com/files/NLJ_SCARFUS.pdf

75.   Heffernan, M. (2015, May). Forget the pecking order at work. *TEDWomen 2015.* Video. Retrieved from https://www.ted.com/talks/margaret_heffernan_why_it_s_time_to_forget_the_pecking_order_at_work.

76.   Groysberg, B., Nanda, A., Nohria, N. (2004, May). "The Risky Business of Hiring Stars." *Harvard Business Review*. Retrieve from https://hbr.org/2004/05/the-risky-business-of-hiring-stars

77.   Sohani, S.S., Varkkey, B. (2015, October). "Breaking Free From the Bell Curve: An Alternate Proposition for Performance Management." *Indian Institute of Management*. W.P. No. 2015-10-04. Ahmedabad, India. Retrieved from http://www.iimahd.ernet.in/assets/snippets/workingpaper-pdf/6096466172015-10-04.pdf

78.   Quoted in: "Facebook's VP of Tech Communications on Building a Bulletproof Comms Strategy.: (n.d.) Retrieved from http://firstround.com/review/facebooks-vp-of-tech-communications-on-building-a-bulletproof-comms-strategy/

79.   Harvard Business Review Staff (2014, November). "How Companies Can Profit from a 'Growth Mindset'." *Harvard Business Review*. Retrieved from https://hbr.org/2014/11/how-companies-can-profit-from-a-growth-mindset

80.   Babiak, P; Hare, R.D. (2007). *Snakes in Suits: When Psychopaths Go to Work*. HarperCollins e-books. Retrieved from http://sttpml.org/wp-content/uploads/2014/06/psycophaths-at-work1.pdf

81.   Babiak, P., Hare, R.D. (2007). *Snakes in Suites: When Psychopaths Go to Work*. HarperCollins e-books. Retrieved from http://sttpml.org/wp-content/uploads/2014/06/psycophaths-at-work1.pdf

82.   Employee Engagement in U.S. Stagnant in 2015. (2016, January 13). Gallup. Retrieved from http://www.gallup.com/poll/188144/employee-engagement-stagnant-2015.aspx

83.   Survey results from Gallup as reported in Crabtree, S. (2013, October 8). Worldwide, 13% of Employees Are Engaged at Work. Retrieved from http://www.gallup.com/poll/165269/worldwide-employees-engaged-work.aspx

𝕱𝕽𝕽

84. Adkins, A. (2015, January 28). Majority of U.S. Employees Not Engaged Despite Gains in 2014. Retrieved from http://www.gallup.com/poll/181289/majority-employees-not-engaged-despite-gains-2014.aspx

85. Adkins, A. (2015, January 28). Majority of U.S. Employees Not Engaged Despite Gains in 2014. Retrieved from http://www.gallup.com/poll/181289/majority-employees-not-engaged-despite-gains-2014.aspx

86. Survey details: "2,004 respondents are 18+ years old, employed full-time, and work for organizations with 100 or more employees....Conducted in October." (2015, Fall). *ModernSurvey Report*. The State of Employee Engagement. Retrieved from http://www.modernsurvey.com/wp-content/uploads/2015/12/The-State-of-Engagement-Report-Fall-2015.pdf

87. Nichols, W.J. (2014, July 19). Why our brains love the ocean. *Salon*. Retrieved from http://www.salon.com/2014/07/19/why_our_brains_love_the_ocean_science_explains_what_draws_humans_to_the_sea/

88. Bor, D. (2012). *The Ravenous Brain: How the New Science of Consciousness Explains Our Insatiable Search for Meaning*. Basic Books. Retrieved from http://boingboing.net/2012/09/24/excerpt-from-the-ravenous.html

89. McGonigal, K. (2011, December 6). How Mistakes Can Make You Smarter. *Psychology Today*. Retrieved from https://www.psychologytoday.com/blog/the-science-willpower/201112/how-mistakes-can-make-you-smarter

90. McGonigal, K. (2011, December 6). How Mistakes Can Make You Smarter. *Psychology Today*. Retrieved from https://www.psychologytoday.com/blog/the-science-willpower/201112/how-mistakes-can-make-you-smarter

91. Brown, B. (2012). "Vulnerability is the birthplace of innovation, creativity and change." *TED2012* Retrieved from http://blog.ted.com/vulnerability-is-the-birthplace-of-innovation-creativity-and-change-brene-brown-at-ted2012/

92.   Interview with Schawebel, D. (2016, August 3). Joel Peterson: How To Build A High Trust Organization. *Forbes*. Retrieved from http://www.forbes.com/sites/danschawbel/2016/08/03/joel-peterson-how-to-build-a-high-trust-organization/#76f2160625c7

93.   Colquitt, J. A., Scott, B.A., LePine, J. A. (2007). "Trust, Trustworthiness, and Trust Propensity: A Meta-Analytic Test of Their Unique Relationships with Risk Taking and Job Performance." *Journal of Applied Psychology*. Vol. 92, No. 4, pp. 909 –92. Retrieved from https://www.ocf.berkeley.edu/~reetaban/triple%20helix/trust%20and%20decision%20making.pdf

94.   Searle, R.; Bachmann, R; Gillespie, N and Weibel, A. (2011, July 5-8). "Organizational Trust: Challenges and Dilemmas." *EGOS*, Conference, Gotenberg, Sweden. Retrieved from http://oro.open.ac.uk/29962/

95.   Survey details: "2,004 respondents are 18+ years old, employed full-time, and work for organizations with 100 or more employees....Conducted in October." (2015, Fall). *ModernSurvey Report*. The State of Employee Engagement. Retrieved from http://www.modernsurvey.com/wp-content/uploads/2015/12/The-State-of-Engagement-Report-Fall-2015.pdf

96.   Tamblyn, T. (2016, March 23). "We Are Beginning To Feel Crushed By The Number Of Work Emails We Get." *Huffington Post UK*. Retrieved from http://www.huffingtonpost.co.uk/entry/we-are-beginning-to-feel-crushed-by-the-number-of-work-emails-we-get_uk_56f2b084e4b08af01be9f9ee

97.   As reported Heussner, K. M. (2010, July 20). Tech Stress: How Many Emails Can You Handle a Day? *ABC News*. Retrieved from http://abcnews.go.com/Technology/tech-stress-emails-handle-day/story?id=11201183

98. Chui, M. Manyika, J. Bughin, J. Dobbs, R. Roxburgh, C. Sarrazin, H. Sands, G., Westergren, M. (2012, July). "The social economy: Unlocking value and productivity through social technologies." *Report - McKinsey Global Institute.* Retrieved from http://www.mckinsey.com/industries/high-tech/our-insights/the-social-economy

99. Research by the University of Glasgow and U.K.-based Modeuro Consulting as reported by Feintzeig, R. (2013, August 9). Before You Hit Send. *Wall Street Journal.* Retrieved from http://blogs.wsj.com/atwork/2013/08/09/before-you-hit-send-read-this/?mod=WSJBlog

100. Mark, G.J., Voida, S., Cardello, A.V. (2012, May). "A Pace Not Dictated by Electrons: An Empirical Study of Work Without Email." *Association for Computing Machinery.* Retrieved from http://www.ics.uci.edu/~gmark/Home_page/Research_files/CHI%202012.pdf

101. Mark, G.J., Voida, S., Cardello, A.V. (2012, May). "A Pace Not Dictated by Electrons: An Empirical Study of Work Without Email." *Association for Computing Machinery.* Retrieved from http://www.ics.uci.edu/~gmark/Home_page/Research_files/CHI%202012.pdf

102. Mark, G., Iqbal, S., Czerwinski, M., Johns, P. (2015, March 14-18). "Focused, Aroused, but so Distractible: A Temporal Perspective on Multitasking and Communications." CSCW '15, Vancouver, BC, Canada. Retrieved from http://www.ics.uci.edu/~gmark/Home_page/Research_files/CSCW%20 2015%20Focused.pdf

103. van de Poll, M.K., Sörqvist, P (2016, May/June). "Effects of Task Interruption and Background Speech on Word Processed Writing." *Applied Cognitive Psychology.* Volume 30, Issue 3. Retrieved from http://onlinelibrary.wiley.com/doi/10.1002/acp.3221/full

104. Txt and email 'reduce IQ more than cannabis. (2005, April 25). *Mail Online.* Retrieved from http://www.dailymail.co.uk/news/article-345878/Txt-email-reduce-IQ-cannabis.html

105.   *Talking Business - Giam Swiegers, CEO Deloitte Australia.* (2011, April 28). Video interview. RMIT University. Retrieved from https://www.youtube.com/watch?v=Vn4Bz8Bm4Fw

106.   Conversation with Judy Hembruff, Toronto, August 2016.

107.   Everything else – all the stuff you can see - is made up of the remaining 5%. Dark Energy, Dark Matter. Science Mission Directorate. (n.d.) *NASA.* Retrieved from https://science.nasa. gov/astrophysics/focus-areas/what-is-dark-energy

108.   Gottfredson, M. (2012, June 28). "The focused company." Bain & Company. *Bain Brief.* Retrieved from http://www. bain.com/publications/articles/the-focused-company.aspx

109.   As quoted in Williams, R. (2012, April 15). Why Meetings Kill Productivity. *Psychology Today.* Retrieved from https:// www.psychologytoday.com/blog/wired-success/201204/ why-meetings-kill-productivity

110.   Johansson, A. (2015, April 8). Why meetings are one of the worst business rituals ever. *Entrepreneur.* Retrieved from https://www.entrepreneur.com/article/244499

111.   "Groupthink [a summary of the thinking of social psychologist Irving Janis, who coined the term]." (n.d.). Prepared by Psychologists for Social Responsibility. Retrieved from http:// www.psysr.org/about/pubs_resources/groupthinkpresenta- tion.ppt.pdf

112.   Hill, N. *Think and Grow Rich.* (n.d.) Retrieved from http:// www.successlearned.com/napoleon-hill-think-grow-rich/files/ basic-html/page19.html

113.   Kim, J-N. (2014, July 2). An Innovative Organization and Its Many Oracles Part II. Blog post. Organizational Communica- tion Research Center. Institute for Public Relations. Retrieved from http://www.instituteforpr.org/innovative-organiza- tion-many-oracles-part-ii/

114.   Dweck, C.S. (2006). *Mindset: The New Psychology Of Success.*

115.   As quoted in Bernstein, M.H. *Regulating Business by Independent Commission.* Princeton University Press. 1955. p. 121. Retrieved from Google Books.

116.   Smith, W.J. (2016, February 14). Expertitis. *National Review.* Retrieved from http://www.nationalreview.com/corner/431312/expertitis

117.   Google Trends. https://www.google.ca/trends/explore?date= all&geo=US&q=%22company%20culture%22

118.   Roberts, S. (2016). *Nimble, Focused, Feisty: Organizational Cultures That Win in the New Era and How to Create Them.* Dallas, Texas: BenBella Books, p. 18.

119.   Thanks to Douglas Hofstadter who, in his book *I Am a Strange Loop* (2007), examines what is consciousness and the meaning of "I".

120.   Dunston, D. (n.d.) Blockbuster: The customer owns your purpose. Blog post. Retrieved from http://daindunston.com/blockbuster-the-customer-owns-your-purpose/

121.   For an examination of how to apply zero-based thinking to your personal life see: How to Use 'Zero Based Thinking' When Making Hard Decisions. (n.d.) *WikiHow.* Retrieved from http://www.wikihow.com/Use-%E2%80%98Zero-Based-Thinking%E2%80%99-When-Making-Hard-Decisions

122.   Reeves, M. Goulet, K., Walter, G., Shanahan, M. (2013, October 21). "Why Transformation Needs a Second Chapter: Lean, but Not Yet Mean." *Boston Consulting Group perspectives.* Retrieved from https://www.bcgperspectives.com/content/articles/transformation_growth_why_transformation_needs_second_chapter_lean_not_yet_mean/

123.   Reeves, M. Goulet, K., Walter, G., Shanahan, M. (2013, October 21). "Why Transformation Needs a Second Chapter: Lean, but Not Yet Mean." *Boston Consulting Group perspectives.* Retrieved from https://www.bcgperspectives.com/content/articles/transformation_growth_why_transformation_needs_second_chapter_lean_not_yet_mean/

124.	Sinek, S. (2012, February 28). Twitter post. Retrieved from https://twitter.com/simonsinek/status/174469085726375936

125.	Shepherd, J. (2011, March 23). Small Firms, Big Lawyers: Why Are You a Small-Firm Lawyer? *Above the Law.* Retrieved from http://abovethelaw.com/2011/03/small-firms-big-lawyers-why-are-you-a-small-firm-lawyer/

126.	Sample of 1,053 adults (300 executives and 753 employees) employed full-time by an organization with at least 100 employees (conducted February 2014). "Culture of Purpose – building business confidence; driving growth." 2014 core beliefs & culture survey. *Deloitte.* (2014). Retrieved from http://www2.deloitte.com/us/en/pages/about-deloitte/articles/culture-of-purpose.html

127.	Bejan, A., Peder Zane, J. (2012). *Design in Nature.* New York: Random House, p. 3.

128.	Transcript, DoD News Briefing - Secretary Rumsfeld and Gen. Myers. (2002, February 12). Retrieved from http://archive.defense.gov/Transcripts/Transcript.aspx?TranscriptID=2636

129.	Wiig, K.M. (2003). "A Knowledge Model for Situation-Handling." White paper. Knowledge Research Institute, Inc. p. 7. Retrieved from http://www.krii.com/downloads/model%20 sit_handling.pdf

130.	Semple, E. (2012). *Organizations Don't Tweet, People Do.* Hoboken, NJ: Wiley.

131.	For more on the cycle and versions of it see https://en.wikipedia.org/wiki/PDCA

132.	Experiential learning cycle. (n.d.) Retrieved from http://health.tki.org.nz/Key-collections/Curriculum-in-action/Making-Meaning/Teaching-and-learning-approaches/Experiential-learning-cycle

133.   Managers Say the Majority of Information Obtained for Their Work Is Useless, Accenture Survey Finds. (2007, January 4). Press release. *Accenture*. Retrieved from https://newsroom.accenture.com/subjects/technology/managers-say-majority-information-obtained-for-their-work-is-useless-accenture-survey-finds.htm

134.   Memorandum to Secretary Walcott re: his son Stuart's grave site; as found in "Evolution of the Memo, 1849-2011." (2011, November 17). *Smithsonian Institute Archives*. Retrieved from http://www.slideshare.net/SIArchives/evolution-of-the-memo

135.   Morrison, A., Parker, B. (2011). "The collaboration paradox: More social information helps the workforce find what it's looking for." *PwC Technology Forecast*. Issue 3. Retrieved from https://www.pwc.com/us/en/technology-forecast/2011/issue3/assets/transforming-collaboration-with-social-tools.pdf

136.   Bejan, A., Lorente, S. (2012). "The physics of spreading ideas." *International Journal of Heat and Mass Transfer*. Retrieved from http://www.academia.edu/15485455/The_physics_of_spreading_ideas

137.   Bejan, A., Peder Zane, J. (2012). *Design in Nature*. New York: Random House.

138.   Chui, M., Manyika, J., Bughin, J., Dobbs, R., Roxburgh, C., Sarrazin, H., Sands, G., Westergren, M. (July 2012). "The social economy: Unlocking value and productivity through social technologies." *McKinsey Global Institute*. Retrieved from http://www.mckinsey.com/insights/high_tech_telecoms_internet/the_social_economy

139.   Kim, E Why investors are throwing money at $2.8 billion startup Slack, when it's only making $30 million. (2015, July 14). *Business Insider*. Retrieved from http://www.businessinsider.com/slack-expects-30-million-revenue-2015-7

140.   Choi, J., Chen, W. (2014). The Busy Person's Guide to the Done List. *iDoneThis*. Retrieved from https://idonethis.com/static/docs/The-Busy-Persons-Guide-to-the-Done-List.pdf

141. Evans, L. (2015, June 19). Why Sharing Your Progress Makes You More Likely To Accomplish Your Goals. *Fast Company*. Retrieved from https://www.fastcompany.com/3047432/work-smart/why-sharing-your-progress-makes-you-more-likely-to-accomplish-your-goals

142. Bhalla, J. (2013, May 8). It Is in Our Nature to Need Stories. *Scientific American*. Retrieved from https://blogs.scientificamerican.com/guest-blog/it-is-in-our-nature-to-need-stories/

143. Haidt, J. (2012, March 13). "The Righteous Mind: Why Good People are Divided by Politics and Religion." Knopf Doubleday Publishing Group. Retrieved from https://books.google.ca/books?id=U21BxGfm3RUC&printsec=frontcover&redir_esc=y&hl=en#v=onepage&q=%22human%20mind%20is%20a%20story%20processor%2C%20not%20a%20logic%20processor%22&f=false

144. Image by Jeff.lasovski. (2014, July 4). Retrieved from https://commons.wikimedia.org/wiki/File:Simple-kanban-board-.jpg

145. Blenko, M. W., Mankins, M. C., Rogers, P. (2010, June). "The Decision-Driven Organization." *Harvard Business Review*. Retrieved from https://hbr.org/2010/06/the-decision-driven-organization

146. Bejan, A., Peder Zane, J. (2011, November 2). Why Occupy Wall Street's non-hierarchical vision is unobtainable. *The Daily Caller*. Retrieved from http://dailycaller.com/2011/11/03/why-occupy-wall-streets-non-hierarchical-vision-is-unobtainable/

147. For some pertinent examples of how the Pointy-haired Boss (PHB) works, see http://www.businessinsider.com/best-pointy-haired-boss-moments-from-dilbert-2013-10#august-2001-1

148. Laurence J. Peter as quoted in Peter principle. (n.d.). *Wikipedia*. Retrieved from https://en.wikipedia.org/wiki/Peter_principle

149. Gladwell, M. (2005). Why Do We Love Tall Men? Excerpt from *Blink*. Retrieved from http://gladwell.com/blink/why-do-we-love-tall-men/

150. Fairchild, C. (2015, January 14). Why so few women are CEOs (in 5 charts). Retrieved from http://fortune.com/2015/01/14/why-so-few-women-ceos/

151. Wallace, G. 2015. Only 5 black CEOs at 500 biggest companies. *CNN Money.* (2015). Retrieved from http://money.cnn.com/2015/01/29/news/economy/mcdonalds-ceo-diversity/

152. What Exactly is God Complex? 2015, December 22. Retrieved from https://nobullying.com/god-complex/

153. Collier, J. (n.d.). "Information dynamics, self-organization and the implications for management." Retrieved from http://web.ncf.ca/collier/papers/Information_dynamics_self-organization_and_management.pdf

154. Sartre as quoted in Talk:Boats (n.d.). Wikiquote. Retrieved from https://en.wikiquote.org/wiki/Talk:Boats

155. Talk:Boats (n.d.). Wikiquote. Retrieved from https://en.wikiquote.org/wiki/Talk:Boats

156. Rogers, P., Blenko, M.W. (2006, January). "Who Has the D?: How Clear Decision Roles Enhance Organizational Performance." *Harvard Business Review.* Retrieved from https://hbr.org/2006/01/who-has-the-d-how-clear-decision-roles-enhance-organizational-performance

157. For more on communicating memes as form of entertainment, see Collier, J., Burch, M. (1998). "Order From Rhythmic Entrainment and the Origin of Levels Through Dissipation." *Symmetry: Culture and Science.* Order / Disorder, Proceedings of the Haifa Congress. Vol. 9, Nos. 2-4. Retrieved from https://www.academia.edu/2986085/Order_From_Rhythmic_Entrainment_and_the_Origin_of_Levels_Through_Dissipation

158. Hawes, L. (2014, June 26). Adaptive Case Management Could Be The Foundation For Networked Business. *Forbes.* Retrieved from http://www.forbes.com/sites/larryhawes/2014/06/26/adaptive-case-management-could-be-the-foundation-for-networked-business/#4c3291f45d12

159. I am indebted to Filip Callewaert, Head of Information and Knowledge Management, Port of Antwerp, for introducing me to this concept.

160. As quoted in William Gibsom. (n.d.). *Wikipedia.* Retrieved from https://en.wikiquote.org/wiki/William_Gibson

161. Employees' Choice Awards: Highest Rated CEOs. United States: 2016. (n.d.) *Glassdoor.* Retrieved from https://www.glassdoor.com/Award/Highest-Rated-CEOs-LST_KQ0,18.htm

162. Sharma, R. (2016, October 6). Tech and Auto Companies Dominate World's Most Valuable Brands List (AAPL, GOOG). *Investopedia.* Retrieved from http://www.investopedia.com/news/tech-and-auto-companies-dominate-worlds-most-valuable-brands-list-aapl-goog/

163. Hooker, L. (2016, February 1). How did Google become the world's most valuable company? *BBC News.* Retrieved from http://www.bbc.com/news/business-35460398

164. Google. Reviews. (n.d.). *Glassdoor.* Retrieved October 25, 2016 from https://www.glassdoor.ca/Reviews/Google-Reviews-E9079.htm

165. How we hire. (n.d.). *Google.* Retrieved from https://www.google.ca/about/careers/how-we-hire/

166. Corporate jobs. (n.d.). *Apple.* Retrieved from https://www.apple.com/jobs/us/corporate.html

167. Jean Giraudoux. (n.d.). *Wikiquote.* Retrieved from https://en.wikiquote.org/wiki/Jean_Giraudoux

168. Pink, D. (2010, April 1). "RSA ANIMATE: Drive: The surprising truth about what motivates us." *The RSA.* Video. Retrieved from https://www.youtube.com/watch?v=u6XAP-nuFjJc

169. Translated by Derek Lin (2006). *The Feminine Tao.* Chapter 63. Retrieved from http://earlywomenmasters.net/tao/ch_63.html

170. Machiavelli, N. (1532). *The Prince.* Retrieved from http://www.constitution.org/mac/prince06.htm

171. Interview with Salim Ismail. (n.d.). Retrieved from https://ingworld.ing.com/en/2015-2Q/11-interview-salim-ismail

172. Buchanan, D. A., (2003, June). "Demands, Instabilities, Manipulations, Careers: The Lived Experience of Driving Change." *Human Relations.* Vol. 56 no. 6, pp. 663-684. Retrieved from http://hum.sagepub.com/content/56/6/663.short

173. As quoted in Restle, H. (2015, August 19). A CEO shares his best advice for getting promoted quickly when you're in your 20s. *Business Insider.* Retrieved from http://www.businessinsider.com/how-millennials-can-get-promoted-2015-8

174. Presentation by Salim Ismail, CEO, ExO Works & Founding Executive Director, Singularity University. (2016, October 27). *TEDxToronto.*

175. As quoted in Abraham Lincoln. (n.d.). *Wikiquote.* Retrieved from https://en.wikiquote.org/wiki/Abraham_Lincoln

176. For more see https://en.wikipedia.org/wiki/Dunning%E2%80%93Kruger_effect

177. Johnson, B. (1998, September). "Polarity Management: A Summary Introduction. Retrieved from http://www.jpr.org.uk/documents/14-06-19.Barry_Johnson.Polarity_Management.pdf

178.   Koller, R. (n.d.). Oversimplifying Change Management. Blog post. Retrieved from http://www.howtochangemanagement. com/2012/12/oversimplifying-change-management.html

179.   Eyal, N. (n.d.). People Don't Want Something Truly New, They Want the Familiar Done Differently. Blog post. Retrieved from http://www.nirandfar.com/2015/06/california-role-rule.html

180.   Jeffrey Goldstein in his book *The Unshackled Organisation,* as quoted in Herrero, L's *Viral Change: The Alternative to Slow, Painful and Unsuccessful Management.* (2008). Meetingminds; 2nd Revised edition

181.   Lawson, E., Price, C. (2003). "The psychology of change management." *McKinsey Quarterly.* Retrieved from http://www. mckinsey.com/business-functions/organization/our-insights/ the-psychology-of-change-management

182.   Purpose. (n.d.). Coca-Cola Bottling Co. Consolidated website. Retrieved from http://www.cokeconsolidated.com/our-company/our-purpose.aspx

183.   Investor Relations. (n.d.). Coca-Cola Bottling Co. Consolidated website. Retrieved from http://phx.corporate-ir.net/ phoenix.zhtml?c=114845&p=irol-index

184.   About Us - Deloitte's Purpose. (n.d.). Deloitte website. Retrieved from https://www2.deloitte.com/us/en/pages/ about-deloitte/articles/gx-purpose-positive-enduring-impact-that-matters.html

185.   Source: Upper Paleolithic artist, derivative trace by Spassov, N., Stoytchev, T. from *Wikimedia Commons.* Retrieved from: https://commons.wikimedia.org/wiki/File%3ACrocuta_crocuta_cave_art_-_Lascaux_cave.png

186.   Wilford, J.N. (2014, October 6). "Cave Paintings in Indonesia may be among the oldest known." *New York Times.* Retrieved from http://www.nytimes.com/2014/10/09/science/ancient-indonesian-find-may-rival-oldest-known-cave-art.html

187.   Widrich, L. (2012, December 4). The Science of Storytelling: Why Telling a Story is the Most Powerful Way to Activate Our Brains. *Lifehacker*. Retrieved from http://lifehacker.com/5965703/the-science-of-storytelling-why-telling-a-story-is-the-most-powerful-way-to-activate-our-brains

188.   Hasson, U. (2010, December). "Defend Your Research: I Can Make Your Brain Look Like Mine. *Harvard Business Review*. Retrieved from https://hbr.org/2010/12/defend-your-research-i-can-make-your-brain-look-like-mine

189.   The Climate Change Reality Project website. (n.d.). Retrieved from https://www.climaterealityproject.org/leadership-corps

190.   The five disciplines of Viral Change. The viral change mobilizing platform. (n.d.) Retrieved from http://www.viralchange.com/the_five_disciplines_of_viral_change.html

191.   As quoted in Williams, R. (2016, May 27). The Psychology of Organizational Change: How Neuroscience Can Help Leaders. *Business.com*. Retrieved from http://www.business.com/management/the-psychology-of-organizational-change-how-neuroscience-can-help-leaders/

192.   McFarland, W. (2012, October 16). "This is Your Brain on Organizational Change." *Harvard Business Review*. Retrieved from https://hbr.org/2012/10/this-is-your-brain-on-organizational-change

193.   Quoted in Heritage Minutes Collection: *Marshall McLuhan*. (n.d.). Retrieved from https://www.historicacanada.ca/content/heritage-minutes/marshall-mcluhan

194.   Peters, T. (n.d.). What gets measured gets done. Retrieved from http://tompeters.com/columns/what-gets-measured-gets-done/

195.   Goldstein, J. (1994). *The Unshackled Organization: Facing the Challenge of Unpredictability Through Spontaneous Reorganization*. Portland, Oregon: Productivity Press. Retrieved from http://216.119.127.164/edgeware/archive/think/main_filing7.html

196.   Source: *The Feminine Tao*. Chapter 63. (n.d.). Retrieved from: http://earlywomenmasters.net/tao/ch_63.html

197.   Memorial: Karl Marx grave - erection date: 1956. (n.d.). London Remembers website. Retrieved from http://www.londonremembers.com/memorials/karl-marx-grave

198.   McChrystal, S. (n.d.). "*Team of Teams* Quotes." Retrieved from https://www.goodreads.com/work/quotes/41976700-team-of-teams-the-power-of-small-groups-in-a-fragmented-world

199.   Goldstein, J. (1994). *The Unshackled Organization: Facing the Challenge of Unpredictability Through Spontaneous Reorganization.* Portland, Oregon: Productivity Press. Retrieved from http://216.119.127.164/edgeware/archive/think/main_filing7.html

200.   Rozovsky, J. (2015, November 17). The five keys to a successful Google team. *reWork*. Blog post. Retrieved from https://rework.withgoogle.com/blog/five-keys-to-a-successful-google-team/

201.   The Emperor's New Clothes."(n.d.). *Wikipedia*. Retrieved from https://en.wikipedia.org/wiki/The_Emperor%27s_New_Clothes

202.   What is Judo? (n.d.). *World Judo Day*. Retrieved from http://www.worldjudoday.com/en/WhatisJudo-57.html

203.   Shapira, P. (2009). *Physical Exercises & the Martial Arts*. New Delhi: Epitome Books. Retrieved from https://books.google.ca/books?id=9uM5id-uMA0C&dq=physical+exercise+martial+arts

204.   Snowden, D. (2014, June 20). Thinking simply, in context. Cognitive Edge. Blog post. Retrieved from http://cognitive-edge.com/blog/thinking-simply-in-context/

205.   Snowden, D. (2014, October 5). Intervening in a complex domain. *Cognitive Edge*. Blog post. Retrieved from https://cognitive-edge.com/blog/intervening-in-a-complex-domain/

206. McChrystal, S. *"Team of Teams* Quotes." Retrieved from https://www.goodreads.com/work/quotes/41976700-team-of-teams-the-power-of-small-groups-in-a-fragmented-world

207. Michael Roehrig, M., Schwendenwein, J., Bushe, J.R. (n.d.) "Amplifying Change: A 3-Phase Approach to Model, Nurture and Embed Ideas for Change." Prepublication version of Chapter 15 in Bushe, G.R. & Marshak, R.J. (eds.) (2015) Dialogic Organization Development: The Theory and Practice of Transformational Change. San Francisco: Berrett-Koehler. Retrieved from http://www.treeisland.com/sites/default/files/documents/brochures-spec-sheets/Amplifying%20Change%20by%20Gervase%20Bushe.pdf

208. J. Habermas, (2001). *Moral consciousness and communicative action.* Cambridge, Mass.: MIT Press as quoted in Mejias, U.A., (2005, March). "Re-approaching Nearness: Online communication and its place in Praxis." First Monday. Volume 10, Number 3–7. Retrieved from: http://journals.uic.edu/ojs/index.php/fm/article/view/1213/1133

209. Mirabela, P. A. (n.d.). Doublespeak an Euphemisms in Business English. Retrieved from http://steconomiceuoradea.ro/anale/volume/2010/n1/018.pdf

210. As quoted in Duhigg, C. (2016). "Endnotes - Smarter Faster Better." Retrieved from http://charlesduhigg.com/wp-content/uploads/2016/06/Endnotes-Smarter-Faster-Better.pdf

211. As quoted in "Guilt, Shame and Vulnerability: 25 Quotes from Dr. Brené Brown." (n.d.) Retrieved from http://cathytaughinbaugh.com/guilt-shame-and-vulnerability-25-quotes-from-dr-brene-brown/

212. Hazy, J.K., Goldstein, J.A., Lichtenstein, B.B. (2007). "Complex Systems Leadership Theory: An Introduction." *Complex Systems Leadership Theory: New Perspectives from Complexity Science on Social and Organizational Effectiveness.* Exploring Organizational Complexity Series, Volume 1. Mansfield, MA: ISCE Publishing. p. 8. Retrieved from http://www.emergentpublications.com/documents/9780979168864_contents.pdf

213.   Kegan, R., Lahey, L. Fleming, A., Miller, M., (2014, April). "Making Business Personal." *Harvard Business Review*. Retrieved from https://hbr.org/2014/04/making-business-personal

214.   Rock, D. (2013, October 23). Why organizations fail. *Fortune*. Retrieved from http://fortune.com/2013/10/23/why-organizations-fail/

215.   As quoted in Hardy, B.P. (n.d.). How to put yourself on a powerful path and avoid regrets in life. *Medium*. Blog post. Retrieved from https://medium.com/the-mission/how-to-put-yourself-on-a-powerful-path-and-avoid-regrets-in-life-a7e5a4be3c88#.v3vrtoryp

216.   Hardy, B.P. (n.d.). How to put yourself on a powerful path and avoid regrets in life. *Medium*. Blog post. Retrieved from https://medium.com/the-mission/how-to-put-yourself-on-a-powerful-path-and-avoid-regrets-in-life-a7e5a4be3c88#.v3vrtoryp

217.   What Is Important Is Seldom Urgent and What Is Urgent Is Seldom Important. May 9, 2014. *Quote Investigator*. Retrieved from http://quoteinvestigator.com/2014/05/09/urgent/

Endnotes

INDEX

Page numbers in italics refer to figures.

GORDON VALA-WEBB is an innovation professional and an award-winning knowledge management practitioner
and thought leader. He has 17 years of experience helping large/
complex public- and private-sector organizations to transform.
He is an author, speaker, and consultant with his own firm.

Previous roles he has held include National Director of Knowledge Management for PwC Canada, National Director of Innovation and Information at McMillan LLP, and Cabinet Office
Policy Advisor (Ontario). He and his teams have won a number
of awards including Jive World's "New Ways in Business" and the
Showcase Ontario Award for Organizational Transformation.

Gordon is on the board of directors of the International
Association of Innovation Professionals and holds a Master's
degree in the Management of Technology. Gordon lives in
Toronto, Canada.

elevate
publishing

DELIVERING TRANSFORMATIVE MESSAGES
TO THE WORLD

Visit www.elevatepub.com for our latest offerings.

NO TREES WERE HARMED IN THE MAKING OF THIS BOOK.

OK, so a few did make the ultimate sacrifice.

In order to steward our environment, we are partnered with *Plant With Purpose,* to plant a tree for every tree that paid the price for the printing of this book.

To learn more, visit www.elevatepub.com/about

PLANT W|TH PURPOSE | WWW.PLANTWITHPURPOSE.ORG